Sent by the Spirit

SENT BY THE SPIRIT

*First-person Accounts about New Kinds
of Community Service, and New Levels
of Caring, for Catholics in the
Charismatic Renewal*

Compiled by
Ralph Martin

PAULIST PRESS
New York/Paramus/Toronto

Library of Congress
Catalog Card Number: 76-5671

ISBN: 0-8091-1946-0

Published by Paulist Press
Editorial Office: 1865 Broadway, N.Y., N.Y. 10023
Business Office: 400 Sette Drive, Paramus, N.J. 07652

Printed and bound in the
United States of America

Contents

Introduction

One of the major preoccupations of the bishops during Vatican II was how to equip the Church to carry out its fundamental mission of bringing the world the Good News of the saving power of Jesus Christ and its transforming effect on human lives and institutions. They knew that this would be no easy task in a society that was increasingly turning its back on the Gospel message.

While many attempts have been made to bring the Gospel message to the world since Vatican II, few of them have succeeded. Many people who are engaged in missionary activity as a full time occupation are disappointed and discouraged because their efforts have borne so little fruit, especially in trying to solve the social problems of our time. Some of these people have given up their missionary work. Others have even left the Church.

In their *Decree on the Apostolate of the Laity,* the bishops at Vatican II called all Catholics to examine their own missionary vocation in the Church. Unfortunately, their call has gone largely unheeded. The mass of ordinary Catholics, as well as many other people who call themselves Christians, have little awareness and even less enthusiasm to carry out their mission as Christians. In the area of evangelization, which the Council Fathers called "the primary goal of the Christian mission," virtually nothing has been done.

However, a spiritual renewal that is sweeping the Churches today offers much encouragement. Through the charismatic renewal, individual Christians and groups of Christians in many localities are examining their call to serve in the Church's mission to the world. Moreover, they are seeing real fruit coming from their efforts to serve.

Why do they encounter so much success where others have failed? I think there are basically three reasons that account for their success. First of all, the Christians who are carrying out this mission have had their own lives transformed by the power of the Holy Spirit. Because of the visible change that has taken place in their lives, their witness takes on added meaning in the eyes of others. Secondly, they are joining together with their brothers and sisters in Jesus Christ in order to carry out their mission. In doing so, they receive the support and encouragement they need in order to persevere. And thirdly, the work that they are doing is being done under the guidance of the Holy Spirit. No longer are their decisions on which field of service to engage in based first and foremost on need alone; their decisions are being made primarily in light of where the Holy Spirit is leading them to exercise their mission as Christians.

The collection of stories in this book, taken from NEW COVENANT, the English magazine which has served the Catholic charismatic renewal for five years presents a remarkable vision of the creativity of the Holy Spirit in leading Christians into a great variety of Christian service. They provide unmistakable proof that the Church cannot carry out its mission effectively unless it does so in the power of the Holy Spirit. They show that, when a body of Christians come alive and are renewed personally and corporately by the Holy Spirit remarkable things will begin to happen. And this is just the beginning.

RALPH MARTIN
Ann Arbor, March 1976

Faith Village:
The Lord's Landlords

By Bob Horning

Every morning at 6:15 the landlords of Faith Village meet for prayer. Among them are a plumber, an electrician, a groundskeeper, a gardener. These aren't their vocations, but are their responsibilities as owners and operators of the apartment complex. They have other full-time jobs.

On August 1, 1973, the 12 covenant members of the Alleluia Community bought and moved into Faith Village, which covers a whole block in downtown Augusta, Georgia. The Lord had called them to live together as a body, and at the same time to serve the existing tenants.

Now community families or members live in half of the 36 apartments. They are learning to live in common and to spread the Gospel by being Christian landlords. They view each trouble call from tenants as a chance to witness to Jesus.

The Alleluia Community had its beginnings around Easter of 1970 when its present leader, Bill Beatty, and his wife were baptized in the Holy Spirit. "Soon afterwards we began meeting in homes with other couples as our desire for a greater commitment to one another grew," Beatty said.

1

"After about two years, we opened the group to others who wanted to have a covenant community relationship." In order to learn what type of community the Lord wanted, they began praying and fasting one day a week. The men went on a retreat in October and felt the group was being called to live together, possibly under the same roof. The women were unfavorable at first, especially since it would mean selling their homes and, for most of them, moving into a smaller place. But after going on a retreat themselves, they came back agreeing with the men, and the whole group began meeting both Friday and Saturday nights to pray and for fellowship. God used this time to purify their hearts and prepare them to live more closely.

Having agreed that they should live together, the next step was to find a place. After a convent, rectory, and some tenements didn't work out, the apartment complex which they later named Faith Village became a possibility.

That looked good, but expensive. They had just turned down the Greene Street tenements offer because it would cost too much—$40,000. Now, if they bought Faith Village, they would be committed to pay $340,000, with the closing money due in a month. They felt the Lord said to go ahead.

Things happened quickly after their decision. Kevin Murrell gave up his medical school tuition as earnest money (two weeks later he received free tuition). Others planned to sell their homes and throw the money into the pot as they were sold, in order to get the closing money. Some of them gave up their summer jobs and began renovating the buildings, trusting that they would accumulate enough money.

The McBride's didn't even advertise that their house was for sale, but someone drove up and offered to buy it. The night before the closing, the Dale Clark's sold their home. Four hours before the closing, the Murrell's sold theirs. That provided the money needed.

When the community members moved in and became landlords, they went to each tenant and told them why they were living together as a community, invited them to dinner, and let them use their tools.

Most of the tenants are black, and the community feels they are to show them that they aren't white landlords who are trying to take advantage of them, but that they are Christians who live together and love and serve their neighbors.

"We are penetrating their lives by our love, and involving them in our lives any way we can," Beatty says. "This happens many ways: two of the tenants who are soldiers pray each morning with the men of the community. A playground is being set up, and free termite and pest control are offered to the tenants. The community has set up a child care ministry for preschool children in the neighborhood." The tenants' rent covers the mortage payments, and the rent of the community members (same amount as tenants) is being used to renovate the buildings and grounds.

Community life has developed rapidly since moving into Faith Village. The covenant members eat together three times a week and also have Eucharist three times a week, which is fully supported and often celebrated by local clergy or the bishop. On Monday, Tuesday, and Wednesday the community prays together; those outside the community are also invited, and ministry for special requests is held each night. Saturdays are family or household days, but often they have impromptu picnics or get-togethers for everyone. They also have a community picnic one Sunday a month to celebrate all birthdays, anniversaries, and special occasions, which may include a bike-hike or outing for the children.

"Different ones of us have turned our special interests into services for the others," Beatty said. "Among other things, we have a vegetable garden, we sell pecans from our pecan trees, operate a tape/book lending library, a community goods room, and an arts-and-crafts center. Our basic attitude is that everybody's goods belong to everybody. We share our clothes and have a car pool. Each household, consisting of one family or of single men or women, is allocated what they think is a reasonable budget for themselves, and what is left over from their income at the end of the month is put into a fund to be used as needed by the community." Besides their own living quarters, the community has an "Alleluia" house which holds the kitchen, dining hall, freezer room, two offices, a chapel, and maintenance shop.

Living together and serving their tenants is a full-time work, but the Alleluia Community also has several outreaches. They sponsor days of renewal for the Augusta area, hold leadership workshops, publish a monthly newsletter and a prayer group directory for the southeastern United States, and host a Thursday night prayer meeting for Augusta, which averages 200 people.

Because of the growth of these outreaches and internal service needs, nine deacons and deaconesses were appointed in April to assume responsibility for them.

A few other ministries have recently developed. One is a lay-witness mission to some of the parishes in their diocese. "This program is having a great spiritual impact on our diocese," Beatty said. "A team of two families and some single people preach at mass, give their testimonies, start home sharing groups, and set up Life in the Spirit Seminars for parish members. In two of the three congregations they have worked in, over half of the members are now baptized in the Spirit. The third parish currently has 60 people enrolled in the seminars as part of their religious education program, and has a Monday night prayer meeting of more than 100 people."

Seven more parishes are waiting to have a Lay-Witness Mission. This program is developing into an evangelization model for the whole diocese, which covers 30,000 square miles—half of Georgia. The Lay-Witness Mission may soon be on statewide educational television, with a priest giving the Life in the Spirit Seminar. There are also plans for a series of five half-hour television programs on the charismatic renewal.

Since the community has received so many requests to serve and teach in the area, Beatty said that they have felt it more practical to set up a program to bring in leaders for a weekend once a month. They will stay at Faith Village with community members and use "Alleluia" house for lectures and discussions.

In order to live together as a community and to do the service they have been called to, personal relationships must be right. This is an area the Lord has been teaching them about right along. Before forming the community, the Lord taught the members to speak the truth in love, Beatty said, "We learned not to let things fester between one another. We learned ongoing, daily forgiveness. Now we live in a spiritual hothouse—being so close, it's a great chance to grow in the Christian life. There is no more individual sin; we have learned that one person's sin affects everyone else."

Beatty believes that what God is doing in the community will have a more and more far-reaching effect. "The Lord has clearly told us that the community will be 'a light on a mountain' and a real sign to the Church of full Christian community—a believable witness that Jesus is Lord."

A Winning Strategy

By Kerry Koller

Christians are confused about how to act in this last half of the twentieth century. Many grew up believing that Christians had no responsibility for the affairs of the workaday world; yet now they are urged to immerse themselves in the world and its cares. Confronted by both directives, they become quickly disoriented. Only by defining the fundamental and normative relationship of the Christian to his world can we avoid this disorientation and begin to articulate a workable and winning strategy for the Christian in dealing with his environment.

Defining Terms

Three Scriptural concepts are especially important here:

1. *The world* (God's creation). Clearly, Scripture teaches that the material creation of God—the cosmos, earth, man, animals, plants, etc.—is good. God created it out of love, he declared that it was good, and he sent his Son—not to condemn it but to save it from utter ruin.

2. *The "World"* (man's sphere of influence). In the New Testament, especially in the Johannine and Pauline writings, "the World" means the domain of man: the domain in which there is something fun-

damentally opposed to the saving love of God. The things of "this World" (the affairs of men and the things we instinctively set our hearts upon) actively compete with God for the hearts of men. St. John cautions the early Christians:

> *You must not love this passing world or anything that is in the world. The love of the Father cannot be in any man who loves the world, because nothing the world has to offer—the sensual body, the lustful eye, and the pride of life—could ever come from the Father, but only from the world; and the world with all it craves for is coming to an end.* (1 John 2:15-17).

The "World" is not merely a serious distraction to one who is trying to love the Father; it is not simply alienated from God, but is overtly hostile to him and his work. St. Paul mentions a "spirit" of this World which opposes the Spirit of God (for example, 1 Cor. 2:12). And Jesus refers to the ruler of this World as his enemy. "The world hates me," Jesus says (John 7:7), and tells his disciples to expect the same. This hatred is expressed in an absolute way in the World's killing of Jesus.

3. *The Kingdom of God.* "The Kingdom of God" is the Scriptural correlate of the "World". The process of salvation consists in the passing away of the World and appearing of the Kingdom of God.

Jesus speaks of "the Kingdom" both as a present reality (in the lives of those who do the will of the Father) and as something to be realized at the end of time. However, both of these dimensions are brought together in the various parables about the

Kingdom of God: the darnel (Matt. 13:24-30), the seed growing secretly (Mark 4:26-29), the mustard seed (Matt. 13:31-32), and the leaven (Matt. 13:33). In each, something is planted and grows to maturity. Similarly, the Kingdom of God, "planted" in the world through the ministry of Jesus, progresses in human history until it reaches completion at some future date.

The Church and the World

To be accurate, any approach to the relationship of the Christian and world must take note of the following fundamental fact: the Christian is immediately and directly related to the Kingdom of God, and only indirectly related to the "World." To set one's heart on the Kingdom of God means to live the fundamental areas of one's life in the Kingdom, and not in the World. What then does this immediate and direct relationship to the Kingdom of God signify? The traditional and essentially correct account, as expressed in the Vatican Council Documents, identifies the Kingdom and the Church. Nevertheless, it is difficult to understand how our lives are directly related to the Church, when most of our activities and decisions occur in the context of the World.

The question can be answered if we focus on the local church instead of the Church universal. As the Council Fathers wrote, the local church is the organic unit of Christianity:

> *This Church of Christ is truly present in all legitimate local congregations of the faithful which, united with their pastors, are themselves*

called churches in the New Testament. For in their own locality these are the new people called by God, in the Holy Spirit and in much fullness (Lumen Gentium, III, 26).

Given the contemporary expression of the local congregation as found in diocesan and parochial structures, this suggestion at first seems of little help. Although they guarantee the essentials of Christian life, these structures hardly provide for its full expression. Not only is it difficult to imagine how they could encompass the essential relationships of life; it is increasingly difficult to see how they could generate full Christian life. How, then, to manifest in our day-to-day lives our essential and immediate relationship to the Kingdom of God?

Charismatic Communities

Fortunately, there exist in the Church today some promising instances of local congregations exhibiting a vibrant and all-encompassing Christian life. The recent emergence of the charismatic renewal communities holds the promise of renewal for all of Christian life. Indeed, the power of the Holy Spirit has given rise to quite a number of functioning —although embryonic—charismatic renewal communities in cities throughout the United States. And although the Church cannot be understood exclusively in terms of these communities, they do provide concrete examples of the Church as the Kingdom of God; they are actual historical instances of what a viable local church might be.

There are a number of important features about such communities: (1) they are non-Utopian—they do not ignore the demands of normal human existence; (2) they are in the World—they neither flee the cities, nor do they shun the material order; (3) their members find power and meaning for their lives in the worship of God and in prayer; (4) they acknowledge and act upon the social demands of the Gospel; and (5) through the exercise of charismatic gifts and ministries, they develop a community order which finds its main expression in love and respect.

Because their basic relationships are lived out in the matrix of Christian community, members of these congregations experience actual behavioral and social changes in their lives. Relating immediately and directly to a *concrete instance* of the Kingdom of God enables them to adopt the values of the Kingdom without being obliged to structure their lived relationships according to the values of the World.

It does make sense, then, to speak of the Christian's immediate relationship to the Kingdom of God. Our original question—how does the Christian relate to the world?—has now become: how does the local church (the Christian community) relate to the "World"? And since Christianity understands itself to have the mission of overcoming the World and establishing the Kingdom, we can put the question this way: what is the right strategy for Christian communities?

Strategy

We are accustomed to think that people ought to be trained *in* the Christian community and sent *out* into the World in order to reform it. But this is just the sort of strategy that eventually leads to the co-optation of the Gospel message. For the object of

Christianity is to replace the World—not to renew or purify it.

I propose the inverse of the ordinary view: that the basic and normative strategy involves maintaining the life of the community and then bringing people from the World into the community. This is, I suspect, a somewhat novel proposal. But if the community is the locus of the new life of the Kingdom, it makes sense that most of its energy be directed inwardly and that its basic commitment must be to its own existence and growth.

The Christian community offers the world a definite alternative to its present form of life. It should express its concern for the world, not by attempting to reform life lived *within* the World, but by bringing people *to* the community, showing them this new form of life, and inviting them to join in. This parallels the strategy of the early Christian churches, which invited people to change their values and ideals, to make Jesus their Lord, to receive his new life, and to share that life with their fellow Christians.

We do not, of course, deny the Christian imperative that communities serve their non-Christian brothers and sisters and involve themselves in contemporary social problems. This imperative, however, is second in the order of Christian priorities. Vatican Council II quite clearly states the *primary* responsibility of the Christian:

> *to promote God's glory through the spread of His Kingdom, and to obtain for all men that eternal life which consists in knowing the only*

true God and Him whom He sent, Jesus Christ.
(Decree on the Apostolate of the Laity, 1, 3).

Generally, Christians have not succeeded at this task. They have for the most part ignored what life together can be like and have spent their energies trying to change things in the sociopolitical order. As a result, most Christians find church life arid and meaningless.

People need a concrete experience of life in Christ. They need a life with a particular group of people who will love them in a nonpolitical and non-exploitive way. The reform of existing political structures will not bring this about. Our hope lies in the growth of local churches, and the existence of charismatic renewal communities points to new possibilities.

A winning strategy for the Kingdom of God necessitates instances of that Kingdom and the openness and boldness to draw others into the new life which is lived there.

What Is Christian Community?

By Steve Clark

God's purpose in creation and redemption was a unity between God and men, and that involves a unity between man and man. The way God is working to bring this about is through the body of Christ, the Church, the unity of men with God and with one another under the Lordship of Christ (Eph. 1)—in other words, the formation of Christian community.

At the end of the second chapter of Acts, we read of community among the first Christians:

> *They devoted themselves to the apostles' teaching and fellowship, to the breaking of bread and the prayers. And fear came upon every soul; and many wonders and signs were done through the apostles. And all who believed were together and had all things in common; and they sold their possessions and goods and distributed them to all, as any had need. And day by day, attending the temple together and breaking bread in their homes, they partook of food with glad and generous hearts, praising God and having favor with all the people. And the Lord added to their number day by day those who were being saved.*

The result of Pentecost was not for each Christian to receive the Spirit, and then with the power of God in him go off on his own and be another Christ. The result was for the Christians to come together in a greater unity than men had ever seen before (Acts 2:42-47).

The greatest evidence of the Spirit that Luke pays attention to was not speaking in tongues or being filled with God's power. The sign of the authentic work of the Spirit, of true Pentecost, is unity among those in whom the Spirit dwells. If the life of the Spirit does not mean forming community, loving, and getting along with the Christians near us who also have received the Spirit, then something is wrong. It is not the power of God.

In the charismatic renewal, the Lord is restoring the life and power that come from our unity with God, and at the same time restoring our relationship to one another as Christians. Unless we have that relationship working right, we will not see the full power of God. That is why we are concerned with Christian community in the charismatic renewal.

Community is not things that you do. It is a relationship that exists among people. Until we are in the right relationship with one another, we cannot have genuine community, even if we do all the right things.

A bond must exist between Christians that is not there when relating with non-Christians. This existed in the early Church, and we should try to recapture it. In Scripture, the term "brother" is reserved for Christians (or Jews) and is never applied to all men. Other Christians are related to us in Christ; nonbelievers are not. To the early Christians, being brothers meant being born of the same father,

being part of the same family. Those who were
Christians were "*born of God*" (John 1:18), they
were "*born of the Spirit*" (John 3:8), they had been
born "*through the living and abiding word of God*"
(1 Pet. 1:23).

Being in Christ together made a difference in
the way they related. There was nothing more important to them than Christ, and everything was affected by being in Christ. As a result, their most important relationships were with other Christians, not
with their fellow countrymen, not with those who
held the same political ideology or who belonged to
the same social class, not even with their family.

It is not until we accept this truth and begin to
relate to other Christians as our brothers because
they are Christians and not for any other reason,
that Christian community is a possibility.

Being brothers also meant that there was a relationship of brotherly love, care, and service. For
most Christians, the relationship is not one of personal love, except maybe with a small group of people. It is more like friendship. There are small
groups of Christians throughout the world who are
getting to know one another and caring for one another, but the basis of their relationship is the fact of
knowing one another. They cannot understand how
it is possible to experience community, love, and affection outside of their small group. We are vic-
timized by our society into believing all relationships
with larger groups have to be impersonal.

The alternative is Christian brotherly love,
which Christians can share with large numbers without having to be impersonal. Because we belong to
each other in Christ it is possible for a Christian

community of thousands to approach each other with warmth and openness, even though members cannot know everyone as well as they will know a few.

New people and guests who come to our community are often taken aback by how openly they are accepted and loved. "Strangers" come up to them and hug them warmly. Other people share intimately with them right away. They feel loved at once. This happens not just between a couple of individuals, but among a whole body of people. New people know that they can relate in a trusting, affectionate way with the whole community. This is possible because we are brothers, because what unites us is deeper and more important than anything else, and because the same Holy Spirit has poured the love of God into both our hearts.

Another part of the relationship as brothers is commitment. Most Christians make a limited commitment to other Christians. They come together for certain activities, but the rest of their lives are private. The right relationship of brothers and sisters in the Lord is different—it means full commitment. It is similar to the commitment we have to our families.

This full commitment comes by our whole lives being in common. The first thing early Christians had in common was the Holy Spirit. But they also had their lives in common. Perhaps the best definition of Christian community is given in Acts 4:32:

"Now the company of those who believed were of one heart and soul, and no one said that any

of the things which he possessed was his own,
but they had everything in common."

That is community. What is mine is yours and
what is yours is mine. Community does not mean
holding all our possessions together. It can mean
that, but it does not have to. It does, however, mean
that in some real way, all that is mine has to be
yours. It has to be shared. I have to recognize that
when you need something, it has to go to you. You
have a right to it.

We have to share spiritually, personally, and
materially—spiritually first of all. For many Christians, their spiritual lives are the last thing they will
share. They never talk about religion, or if they do,
not in a personal way. They will never tell their
brother that they love the Lord, that he spoke to
them in prayer, or that they sensed his presence in a
strong way. Yet that kind of sharing is a great
source of spiritual benefit. It encourages and brings
life. If we do not share our spiritual goods, we are
hoarding something that is meant to belong to our
brothers also.

We have to share personally. In the modern
world, we are taught to live individualistically. This
means that we are not honest with many people,
usually only with those we have grown to trust. If I
sin, or have a sexual temptation, I am not supposed
to tell anyone. If I am having a hard time with guilt
feelings, I would do my best to hide them. Yet that
is me, and if I have not shared those things, I have
not shared honestly, I have kept my life from my
brothers.

We have to share financially and materially. All

my possessions belong to my brother. Brothers ought to lend to their brother whatever he needs, they ought never take interest, they ought to let him go if he cannot pay (Deut. 15). A traveling Christian ought to know that our house is his house. Christians ought to do these things for one another just because they are Christians. Again, this does not necessarily mean holding our finances or possessions together. But it does mean having a way so that our brother can have access to what he needs.

When we share, the body of Christ becomes more complete. An individual can never be a complete Christian. The only complete Christian is a "body," the Christian community in a particular place. The same thing can be seen from Paul's teaching on spiritual gifts. God distributes the spiritual gifts differently to different people. Since Jesus himself, none of us has had all the workings of the Spirit so that we can act with full power on our own. In every locality there should be a body of people who have all the power Jesus had, who can do, as a body, all the things Jesus did—and greater things.

But this means that we have to be a body. We cannot be a number of individuals functioning on our own. We have to become interdependent. Many of us have difficulty with interdependence, because we were raised to function individualistically. We associate that with being an adult, with being strong. We make our own decisions, chart our own course.

For me to change, I had to let go of my rebellion and independence. I did not want anyone to tell me what to do, and I had to learn that that was acting in the character of Satan, not in the character of Jesus.

Being part of the body of Christ means that your whole life belongs to your brothers and sisters. We cannot be the body of Christ on limited commitments. It would be strange if one of our organs, say, the liver, made only a partial commitment to the body. It would, moreover, be dangerous if the body could not call upon the liver at any time of need. All of our life has to belong to the body. That does not mean that we have to spend all of our time together with members of the community. The members of our community have a normal family life and normal occupations. But their commitment is a full commitment. All of their lives are involved in our commitment together as Christians.

Being part of a body means that none of us can make decisions about our lives on our own. There is an order to the life in a body. Part of that order means that the members have to be subordinate to the life of the body as a whole, and to the direction of the head. The main function of the head is to allow the body to work in interdependence.

Effective authority and subordination are crucial for a successful community. And that subordination has to be personal subordination. Many of us are willing to be subordinate insofar as we are participating in the activities of a particular group, but we are not willing to be subordinate in our personal lives. We have not really put our lives in common, if our lives are not subject to the decisions of the community. The heads of the community are those to whom the community has entrusted its supervision of what has been put in common. Therefore, community does not work if we are not subordinate to the heads.

Subordination does not always imply obedience in everything. It is possible, as our community in Ann Arbor does, to have all decisions subordinated to the head without there being a commitment to obey in everything. For example, if a person were trying to decide whether to marry or not, he would submit the decision to his head, but he would not have to simply accept the head's advice.

A community working right is the source of power to bring Christ to the world. The unity among Christians should lead the world to see the reality of Christ and come to faith in him. Jesus said in John 17:20:

> *I do not pray for these only, but also for those who believe in me through their word, that they may all be one; even as you, Father, are in me, and I in you, that they also may be in us, so that the world may believe that you have sent me.*

The Lord is leading his people all over the world to a point of decision. He is leading us to decide that the Lord Jesus is the most important thing in life and that we have to refound our lives and our relationships on that basis. He is telling us that we have to form deeply committed community with those who have sold out to Christ. It is when we take that radical step that we will begin to see the body of Christ again in the power that God has for it.

Liberation

By Fr. James Burke, O.P.

A word that is heard with increasing frequency in the poor nations of the world and among the minority groups of the rich nations is "liberation." The word expresses an ever deepening hunger of the "wretched of the earth" to be free of all economic, social, cultural, and political oppression, and to share more equally in the earth's blessings.

The majority of the earth's population are marginal persons—men, women, and children living on the margin of society, "ill-fed, inhumanly housed, illiterate, and deprived of political power as well as the means of acquiring responsibility and moral dignity" (*Justice in the World*, Synod of Bishops, 1971). Flagrant injustices have built such a network of domination, oppression, and abuses, that, for these masses of people, freedom is an empty word.

Time is not bringing a solution to the problem. Rather, the gap separating poor from rich is growing constantly wider: the poor are becoming poorer and the rich, richer.

Today, when men speak of liberation, they are usually referring to the work of radically changing the unjust structures, systems, and institutions responsible for the present enormous inequities existing in the world, so that men and nations may be truly free from oppression.

It would be truly difficult to overestimate the strength of the desire for liberation among the poor people of the world. There is little that happens in underdeveloped countries that cannot be explained by the longing for liberation. The liberation movement, however, is not confined to the poor nations. In the most advanced countries, countless men and women struggle to be free from oppressive structures. Young people and minority groups feel enslaved by "the establishment." Millions are burdened by the new loneliness of urban civilization where man feels himself a stranger in an anonymous and indifferent crowd. Technology seems to have slipped from man's control to hurtle aimlessly on, threatening to make the environment inhospitable for man, and even for life itself. In these areas and many more, affluent societies are seeing movements of liberation growing stronger day by day.

In my retreat work in the United States and Latin America, I have heard repeatedly one criticism of the charismatic renewal: that its members are not involved in the work of liberation, but have an individualistic spirituality which is an escape from the real world and its enormous problems. My experience with the charismatic renewal does not confirm this. I believe that the yearning for liberation in the hearts of men and women all over the world is basically the movement of the Spirit of God, but that the Spirit, who leads to all truth, has much to teach the disciples of Jesus regarding liberation.

True Liberation

The Father wants all to share as brothers in the riches of his universe. The present huge disparity between those who live in misery and those who live in affluence is not in any way the will of the Father; nor are the systems and structures that perpetuate such disparity. The Father does not will that his children be oppressed, but wants all to enjoy the perfect freedom of the sons of God. The movement to break down oppressive structures both in poor and rich nations is of the Spirit, though the violence and hatred that sometimes accompany the work of liberation cannot be attributed to the Spirit. He is the wind that is stirring the hearts of men to free themselves from structures that dominate and oppress.

Though the Spirit is moving powerfully to a radical transformation of unjust structures, his work in liberation is more basic. Both Medellin and Che Guevara said that a new society requires new men. A change in structures alone will not eliminate oppression. It will only make for different oppressors and oppressed. For true liberation, there must be a transformation of the heart of man.

Jesus came in the power of the Spirit to liberate man. He denounced enslaving structures and institutions (Matthew 23), but he did much more—he liberated the individual person from oppression: from the forces of nature, from hunger, from sickness and death, and especially from the oppression of sin.

Jesus saw selfishness, fear, worry, greed, bitterness, hatred, and sensuality as the most powerful forces enslaving man, and he liberated man from their oppression through his obedience to his Father and his love for all men. It led him to the cross where he bore the weight of our oppressions.

On Pentecost, Jesus transformed the hearts of his disciples, and they were new men—liberated from fear, ambition, ignorance, and selfishness. Men with new life, new hope, new power rushed to the marketplace, filled with the presence and the love of the Risen Lord, to proclaim the Good News and lift the weight of oppression from the hearts of men.

Jesus' work of liberation goes from the inside out, not from the outside in. He wants to liberate men and nations from unjust structures, but a new society demands new men; it is only the Lord, who has been victorious over all oppression, who can, through his indwelling presence, regenerate man, transform his heart, teach him truly to love, and guide him in the work of liberation. *"If the Son makes you free, you will be free indeed"* (John 8:36).

The love of Jesus is the source of liberation. If we love the oppressed and hate the oppressor, we don't love the oppressed enough to liberate them. Rather, our hatred enslaves us and those we wish to liberate. This has been verified too often in Latin America to be disputed. We've seen men take power in Latin America with the best of intentions. In a few months or a year, the country is in the same state of oppression, despite the good intentions. No one can liberate another unless he himself is free. Liberation has to begin with a renewed heart, a truly liberated man, or liberation on all the other levels of life will not work. Good will is not enough.

There is a restlessness in Latin America today that is explosive. About 90 percent of the young people see the great enemy of their countries as imperialism, the imperialism of the Giant of the North, the United States. They see the salvation of their countries in some form of socialism. They want a just society; they know that that will put them in conflict with the United States business interests that now dominate their social and economic life, but they are determined to bring about the changes that will result in a just society.

Some, perhaps most, cannot see this happening without violent revolution: many young priests are advocating violence. The question that needs to be asked is whether this will bring about real liberation. The external freedom that comes from hatred and violence leaves a man as bound as any external oppression ever could. If you do not love your former oppressor, you are not really free—you will become the new oppressor, not only of those who were in control before, but also of those you set out to free. Slavery to sin is slavery; slavery to hatred is slavery: if you teach someone to hate, you have enslaved him. The true liberation of South America will be through revolution, but it will have to be a revolution of love: all of my own experience has convinced me of it.

The work of liberation needs free men, new men, loving men. Che Guevara, in his diary (It is an amazing book which ought to be read by everyone who considers himself part of the revolution.), shows more concern about the human weaknesses of the members of his guerilla group than about the Bolivian army that was hunting him down. He was very much aware that the unkindness, sensuality, gluttony, and harsh language of the individuals of his band endangered not only the success of their mission, but their very survival. In all his experience, he saw the need of "new men." But in spite of his great leadership qualities he could not transform the hearts of his *guerrilleros*. Only repentance, conversion, and faith in Jesus as Savior and Lord can change the heart of a man. Che sees in his fellow liberators potential oppressors, and worries that his liberation will only be a new form of slavery: he saw that without a change in the essential human misery, changes of structure would have no real effect. I know, by experience, that the only true liberation is in Jesus. Only the Holy Spirit can give a man a heart to serve his people. Without the deep liberation from sin and fear and hatred, there is no true liberation for anyone, and no real revolution, only a shift in power.

True Prophets of Liberation

Jesus drove the money-changers from the temple with a whip, but his love for those who hated him and oppressed his people moved Matthew to recall the words of Isaiah:

> *He will not break the crushed reed, nor put out the smouldering wick* (Matthew 12:20).

This has to be a criterion for discerning the true prophet of liberation from the false. There are many false prophets in South America today, pushing and shouting for different kinds of bold action for liberation. Usually, what they are calling for is basically sound, but they lack the full human sensitivity, so much part of Jesus' ministry, which would make them true liberators.

For example, that nationalization of major industries will be an essential part of the economic liberation of South America few serious people will question. We have seen nationalization, though, which was not liberating. If the country in question does not have the resources to maintain production or keep the markets open, nationalization is not liberation. For many it has meant starvation. The ordinary people supposedly being liberated have been thrust into even deeper poverty; though the "liberators," the ones who initiated the changes, have not gone hungry.

The great longing in the heart of Jesus is to bring his kingdom to earth, to liberate the universe from all oppression.

> *"The whole creation is eagerly waiting for God to reveal his sons . . . creation still retains the hope of being freed like us, from its slavery to decadence, to enjoy the same freedom and glory as the children of God"* (Rom. 8:19-21).

To discover his place in the Father's plan of liberation, the disciple of Jesus looks to the Lord rather than to his own reasoning. "Lord, what is it that you want me to do to free your people and all your creation?"

In his plan of liberation, the Father wants his children to be prophets. A prophet is one who does not form his judgments of situations and people by reading the newspaper or by his own human reasoning, but rather looks to the Father and gets his word.

Today in Latin America, there is great discouragement. Past experience of unsuccessful development efforts lessens hope in future projects. In this state of general dejection, the voice of a prophet of God is being heard. Bishop Eduardo Pironio looked to the Father about the situation in Latin America and, in the Medellín documents, speaks the Father's beautiful word of hope. "A new day is dawning in Latin America." What God sees is not what man sees.

In the world today, there is a new awareness of the oneness of the human family, and a new realization that if one person is oppressed, all are less free. And there is a mighty wind of the Spirit blowing all over the world, moving the children of God out of the slavery of oppression into the full liberty of the sons of God. There is a new day dawning in Latin America. It will be a day of liberation: true liberation in the power and love of Jesus. The Lord will need *his* sociologists, economists, and social psychologists, but it is only he that can free Latin America, and all of us, from oppression.

Christmas in the Dump

By Fr. Rick Thomas, S.J.

In the middle of December, during our Bible study at the Center, we came across this passage in Luke:

> *Then Jesus said to his host, "When you give a dinner or a banquet, do not invite your friends or your brothers or your kinsmen or rich neighbors, lest they also invite you in return, and you be repaid. But when you give a feast, invite the poor, the maimed, the lame, the blind, and you will be blessed, because they cannot repay you. You will be repaid at the resurrection of the just"* (Luke 14:12-14).

We had to ask ourselves if we had ever done this. When do Christians carry out this simple thing that Jesus told us to do when we have a little party? We decided then that we should go to the poorest we knew on Christmas day and share our Christmas meal with those that live on the city dump in Juarez.

As the time drew nearer, we decided to gather at eleven o'clock on Christmas morning. Each person was to bring something for himself to eat and something to share with the poor. When the day finally arrived, five other car-loads of people appeared and we set off with 120 burritos, some tamales, some chocolate milk and some fruit, and crossed the border into Mexico. As we were waiting in Juarez for two more cars to join our caravan, a man came out of a dental shop and shouted, "What are you looking for?" I shouted back, "Jesus, the Lord!" He answered, "He's not here, he's in Russia. What are you looking for?" I said, "Jesus, the Lord!" He said, "We don't need Jesus, we need money!" With that, he went on about his business. Eight cars proceeded out to the city dump.

We were going with some apprehension, not knowing how we would be received or exactly what would happen. The people of the dump had no suspicion that this day would be any different from any other day as they try to scratch out a living by going through the trash on the dump. When we got to the dump, we found, to our dismay, people divided into two factions, not on speaking terms with each other. The dump was divided in half. One group lived and worked on one part and one group lived and worked on the other part. Neither group could enter the territory of the other group.

We were at a loss to know how to have our party with both factions. As we began to ask God to heal the rift, we walked back and forth through the garbage between the two groups trying to work out a compromise or reconciliation. After about a half hour of praising the Lord and compromising, we decided on some neutral territory. The people gathered on either side of a large table, still separated into two camps and hostile.

We told them that we had come to be with them on Christmas day. This was the day Jesus was born,

in love. We were going to sing his praises for a while:
then if anyone was sick we would pray with them for
healing because Jesus liked to heal. We began with
"Bendito," a hymn very familiar to Catholics in
Mexico. As we sang, the Lord began to work and
the people softened. When it came time to pray for
the sick, the people crowded around, forgetting their
barriers. We prayed for a large number of them.

As we were about to begin the meal, the people
lined up to receive a "gift." We told them that we
had not come to give them anything, we had come to
share our dinner with them. This is the difference between taking a Christmas basket to a poor family,
and sharing Christmas dinner with them or inviting
them to your dinner: we all began to experience a
friendliness and an at-homeness. We had expected
and brought food for 120 people. About 250-300
showed up. We told the people that we didn't have
enough for everyone but we would share what we
had brought. They said, "Let the children eat first,
before anyone else." Asking God's blessing, we
began to eat. Somehow there was enough for everybody. Many who were there said that God had simply multiplied the tamales. The people got their
food, we sat down on the ground, and had our little
Christmas meal together. When the meal was over
they went back to work, going through the garbage.

Sharp as these criticisms are, they had remained, for me, rather abstract, until this Christmas.
Then, like Scrooge, I was transported to another
world and given a glimpse of the logical consequences of my way of life. Instead of the gleaming
ornaments on our tree I saw miles of shining tin
cans.

The smell of burnt garbage filled our noses and throats. The sun silhouetted the people of the dump. From a distance, they looked like farmers bent over their rakes and hoes. We came closer, and saw that these were tillers of the garbage, not the soil. Their faces were black and lined with dirt. Their ragged clothes were not enough to protect against the cold. Here and there were open sores and cuts, and one child shivered badly with a fever.

It was incredibly depressing. I looked around for some familiar sight to reorient myself, but there was none. No green tree, no well-dressed children, no laughing—only miles of dump, as far as I could see. On the ground, by my feet, was trash that could have been mine.

What surprised me, though, was the realization that my trash was not just scattered on the ground, but looking at me from large brown eyes. My trash must also be counted in terms of human beings. Somehow, through a process that was kept hidden and remote, my waste produced the people of the dump. My way of life set up a chain of events that ended with the dump and the people of the dump. Here was my brother, a farmer of my garbage. I created his job for him, and I keep him in it.

How merciful the Lord is, for revealing this to me. There were more revelations.

How perfectly the dump people mirrored our society! How clearly our values and behavior were reflected, for as we arrived, the dump people were divided into two opposing groups. Neither was speaking to the other or allowed to cross to the other side. Somehow, I expected the poor to be saints. After all, they have nothing else to do. But they are also suffering with sin, and they live surrounded with ours.

Later, we toured the outskirts of the dump where tiny houses of tin cans and cardboard were built. Here a man would have his shop set up, his property line marked off by a fence of rusted bed-springs. He would be sitting outside the door of his "house" surrounded by his "wealth"—a mound of cans here, bottles there, rags over there. He kept a sharp watch to see that none robbed him. I reflected on how much time I spend on what really is garbage, and, like this man, I care for my trash and keep it company to see that it remains safe.

We took a stroll through the dump and visited some of the people, going from house to house, talking to them. The houses were made out of tin cans and trash that they had collected. I asked one lady, who was sitting between her two daughters on the tin cans, where her house was. She said, "Right here," pointing to a piece of plastic like a garbage bag lying on top of the cans. The other people had a little roof, raised a few inches or a few feet above the cans, that they could crawl under. All this lady had was a piece of plastic on top of the cans that she could either lie under or lie on: that was her home.

As we wandered around we saw a mother nursing a baby, about five months old. The Lord let us know that we should baptize this baby, because it was very sick. The mother told us that the girl's name was Anita. There is no water in the dump, so we sent one of our people to get some so that we could baptize Anita. He brought back a wet hand-kerchief, and I squeezed the water on her head and baptized Anita in the name of the Father, and the

Son, and the Holy Ghost. The mother was very happy that her daughter had become a Christian on this Christmas day.

It was getting to be late in the afternoon. One of the women said, "I have to go home now." I pointed to the dump and said, "This is your home." She said, "Yes, I know, but the rest of my family hasn't realized it yet." All of us had come to a feeling of oneness with the people on the dump. We'd spent time walking around in the same trash that they did, eating the same food that they were eating, talking to them face-to-face, and praying with them about their very real problems.

During dinner an apparently severely retarded boy about 11 years old was brought to us. He had not had a bath for a long while. He was caked with soot and his hair was matted. Also, he had never spoken in his life. As Sr. Mary Virginia approached him, the boy moved away. She said, "I command you, in Jesus' name to come back." He came, and she and I prayed with him. As we were about to leave, some of our group met the dumb boy, and prayed with him again. One of them started to coach him, "Say, 'ah.' " The boy said "ah," and ran down the hill shouting, "ah, ah, ah." By the beginning of March, he had learned his first three words—"yes," "look," and "what."

When we got back to the Youth Center, we prayed together for a while. A 16 year-old girl prayed aloud, "Lord, I thank you for letting me go to the dump today and see the real meaning of Christmas. Now I know that if you had been born today, you would have been born in the dump."

The people who went to the dump were profoundly moved. They were moved by the misery in which these other people lived. They were moved by their humanity and their nobility in all their poverty, trying to scratch out a living in the free enterprise system. They were moved by how the power of God healed the rift between the two factions, and brought them together on Jesus' birthday. They were moved by the physical healings that occurred when Jesus' healing power touched people. Our lives were changed: we will never be the same.

Much more has happened since. People wanted to return to the dump again, and we did, to bring food and clothing and pray with the people. About two weeks after Christmas, 30 of the adult members of our prayer groups made a covenant agreement to live our lives together in the Lord. Now, every week, usually on Saturday, 30 people drive out to the dump. The weather has been awful—snow, wind, rain, cold—but has not changed the attendance. In February, we began to work on housing. Adobe is the common building material in the Southwest, and we are making bricks on location. Small houses will replace the cardboard shacks. In March we joined the people on the dump in planning a food cooperative.

Food and clothing and housing deals with some of the need: prayer is beginning to deal with others. There have been a number of striking physical healings. We have also prayed in faith for a well somewhere nearby, so that these people may have water. God is going to do something great. He is forming a body to bring his word into that situation with power. There will be a miracle.

A Personal Reflection, by Mrs. Jean Soto

(Mrs. Soto is a member of the El Paso prayer group.)

The visit to the dump was the occasion of a new understanding of many things.

Like many others, I had heard that our society is very wasteful. I had read that every person in the U.S. throws out 11 pounds of garbage a day. We see the effects of our carelessness in our polluted environment. We are accused of being a society of fat, uncaring consumers, interested only in our own comfort, and anxious to be protected from any unpleasantness.

How stripped of the familiar protections these dump people were. No education, money, or resources of any kind (except for my garbage). How shocking to find out that they were still human. That means that underneath all this I must be human, too.

I pray that the tender Lord of heaven and earth, who was himself a man, will now reveal to us a way to follow him by serving our new-found brothers.

A Miracle, by Frank Alarcon

(Mr. Alarcon is a member of the El Paso prayer group.)

I witnessed a multiplication of food on Christmas day.

I had doubts we had enough food for the 250 to 300 people who were there. I told Mrs. Villalba that the kids were filling up sacks and boxes of food and that we were going to run out.

I got on top of my truck to see what was happening. On the tailgate were two boneless hams. One lady kept cutting the ham till she tired, and handed the knife to Louie Urrutia. The ham got smaller, but, oh, so slowly.

Finally, everyone had a big piece of ham. Pockets were stuffed with food and children were carrying sacks away. I hollered to Jean Soto, "Where's all this food coming from?"

On the way home we had enough left over to stop by and leave some at the orphanage.

Every time I think about it I get goosebumps all over.

Miracles in a
Garbage Dump

By Cindy Conniff

Fidela, "faithful one," died on December 26, 1973 at the Juarez garbage dump. About 30 co-workers attended her concelebrated Mass in the local church amid balloons, a poinsettia, and plastic flowers from the recent Christmas celebration. Twenty-seven years old, she died of tuberculosis, a disease affecting almost all the men, women, and children among whom she lived and worked at the dump.

A year ago Fidela's death would have merited little attention: in Juarez, where 45 priests serve 600,000 people, certainly not a concelebrated Mass at the city dump. Nor would 30 people have left their work—sorting trash—to attend her funeral. What has happened at the dump to account for the growing unity of those who live there?

On Christmas Day, 1972, members of the El Paso, Texas, prayer group drove the short distance from El Paso to Juarez to share their dinner with those living on the dump. They did so in response to the Gospel of Luke:

Then Jesus said to his host, "When you give a

dinner or a banquet, do not invite your friends or your brother or your kinsmen or rich neighbors, lest they also invite you in return and you be repaid. But when you give a feast, invite the poor, the maimed, the lame, the blind, and you will be blessed, because they cannot repay you. You will be repaid at the resurrection of the just" (Luke 14:12-14).

In describing "Christmas at the Dump" in the May, 1973 issue of *New Covenant*, Father Rick Thomas, S.J., stated that "God is going to do something great. He is forming a body to bring his word into that situation with power. There will be a miracle."

Since then Father Thomas, director of Our Lady's Youth Center which serves one of the poorer sections of El Paso, believes there has been "one miracle after another." He sees this not only as an emerging self-awareness of those at the dump, but also in the deeper commitment to the poor developing within the El Paso and Juarez prayer groups. Some from the prayer groups spend all their free time—20, 30, or 40 hours a week—either at the dump or doing work specifically related to it, such as sorting clothes and packaging food. Recently the leaders established three committees to coordinate the expanding activities of the store, education, and aid to the sick.

The Store

The people on the dump eat the food they pick from the garbage. With the few cents they earn sorting trash, they supplement their diet with one or two staple items such as flour or beans. In March, 1973, the prayer groups and those on the dump organized a food cooperative which now serves 87 families at an initial fee of 80 cents.

Every Saturday afternoon a Dodge Maxi-van loaded with 3,000 pounds of food turns off the main road and heads over the garbage in search of a clear level spot. (The site for this mobile store varies according to where the garbage has been dumped most recently.) Setting up an awning off the back of the truck, the five or six store workers put up counters on three sides to hold the 20 or so staple products. Items such as onions, chilies, soap, rice, flour, and beans, bought at wholesale houses during the week, now sell below cost to members of the cooperative. The store, which sells out in three or four hours, operates at a loss of $100 a week.

By December, 1973, the Dodge, a gift to the prayer group, could no longer carry the increasing quantity of groceries. So in January another van, also a gift, began hauling a portion of the food each Saturday.

Education

A census conducted by the education committee from Juarez revealed that 114 families live and/or work at the dump. (Some people live at the old dump, where they've built adobe houses, and commute to the new garbage site.) About 111 men, 110 women, and 300 children earn their living by sorting the trash and selling it to one of two unions for recycling. The census information will assist endeavors such as the food coop to plan and expand its work.

The education committee supports services offered by other groups or individuals. Recently a nurse, a Sister of Charity, began teaching women at the dump how to care for themselves during pregnancy. Most of the women had no understanding of the development of the fetus and were unaware of the special needs of their bodies during pregnancy. The nurse, who hopes to work regularly at the dump, also plans to conduct a course there for midwives.

A philosophy student from a nearby university attempted to teach reading but found that the children were literally unable to learn, probably because their diet does not provide enough nutrients for adequate brain development. Instead she now teaches basic personal hygiene. Picking through garbage each day regardless of rain, cold, high winds, or heat, damages the hands of the dump workers. Open sores and infections form easily and spread to other parts of the body simply by rubbing an eye or wiping one's mouth. For the time being, the former reading teacher is showing the people how to care for their hands by washing them and rubbing them with cream.

None of the activities at the dump, however, have lasting value apart from the primary task of the education committee: evangelization. On a daily basis members of the prayer group teach, pray with, and read Scripture to the people on the dump. They proclaim the Lordship of Jesus in the midst of such desolation because he alone is the source of life and freedom. Their evangelization provides the foundation and context for the changes occurring at the dump.

Committee for the Sick

The committee for the sick pray with the ill and take those who need medical attention to a doctor. Because of the unsanitary conditions and the lack of qualified personnel, no clinic has been established at the dump. Those who are critically ill are transported to one of the few doctors in Juarez who will treat them without charge.

Available 24 hours a day, members of this committee also assist at times of death. For example, when Fidela died they helped her neighbors on the dump build a coffin, locate a burial site in Juarez and arrange a Christian funeral.

For years, efforts to relieve the misery of those on the dump yielded few results. Now results are being seen. Reflecting on the past year Father Thomas noted that "When the Lord takes over, anything can happen. If we had planned all that's developed since 1972, we'd never have been able to carry it out. Personally, for me it's been a lesson in reading God's Word, taking it seriously and letting the Lord do what he wants."

Lord, Use This Home

By Sir Thomas and Lady Lees

Post Green is the home of Sir Thomas and
Lady Lees and their family. A former posting station in the days of mail coaches, their three-story
Georgian mansion is located on a farm just outside
the English seaside resort of Poole. With its large
garden, trees, and view of the harbor, it would seem
the ideal country retreat—a haven of relaxed and
leisurely living.

And yet, Post Green is not just another lovely
estate. A number of years ago, Tom and Faith Lees
opened their home to the love and power of God,
placing it completely at his disposal for whatever he
might want to accomplish there. Since that time,
Post Green has become a place of hospitality,
prayer, counsel, and healing. It is now a center for
Christian renewal, with a special aim to training
teachers and evangelists through its conferences,
summer camps, and tape and film ministry.

Here, Tom and Faith describe what happened
when they gave the Lord full control over their
hearts and their home.

The Lees are active in their church, where Tom
is a lay reader, an ecumenical officer for the Diocese
of Salisbury, and a member of the General Synod of
the Church of England. He and Faith have four chil-

dren: Sarah, Christopher, Bridget, and Elizabeth.

Tom: I can't really remember a time when I didn't know Jesus. But that is not to say that I was ever truthfully committed to that understanding of him. Although I have always been aware of Jesus as a guide and an influence in my life, I didn't really see the need to make my own open statement of commitment until Faith got converted about 15 years ago.

Faith: At that time, we were helping Tom's mother to make little religious plays and films. But despite my involvement, I was going through a particularly difficult period. Overfatigue and anxiety neurosis had driven me to the brink of a nervous breakdown.

Finally, I sought help at a Church of England center for evangelism, where someone suggested that I let God into my life to cope for me. "I might as well try it," I thought. And God did it: he healed me and changed me.

As I realized that God was a personal God, I was able to teach people about him, about loving him and serving him in a way that I hadn't known anything about. Consequently, I had affect on the parish. God changed the direction of my life and obviously changed me as a person as well. I think that's what affected Tom and a number of other people in the village. That made Tom commit himself openly to God, so that we both became real leaders in spiritual things in the parish for five or six years.

Tom: As we opened our hearts to God, he showed us a new dimension of loving. We had always lived in a sort of open house situation, with the front door open to friends, overseas students, and visitors in general. One day, we received a couple into our house for whom the only answer seemed to be divorce. We just knew that this was wrong, and we believed in the Lord for a miracle—that's the only way I can put it.

Faith: We entered a new dimension of believing God. As we prayed, we kept on asking: "What would Jesus have done in this situation? How would he have advised?" And within a week, the miracle had happened. This couple had given their lives to Christ and asked him into their situation.

Tom: And I think it was during that week that Faith was baptized in the Holy Spirit. She at that time received what I can only describe as gifts of wisdom, understanding, and faith to trust God for the miracle. I myself felt the power of God and watched amazed as I saw him work in this situation. But not until nine months later did I have an experience similar to my wife's.

Faith wanted me to invite an acquaintance of hers, an Anglican priest, to supper. I was very unwilling, but finally I rang him up and said: "Faith wants me to ask you to supper. Would you like to come?" very ungraciously. But he accepted and when he came, I saw in him someone so full of joy and happiness that my first question to him was to ask what made him so different. He replied that the Lord Jesus had baptized him with the Holy Spirit.

As we ate supper, he described this experience and showed me its scriptural basis. I put down my knife and fork and knelt down at the dining room table. "I want this too," I said. "Will you pray with me?" As the priest prayed and laid his hands on my head, I experienced a complete joy and peace. I just felt like giggling and was so happy that I really didn't want any more supper.

That evening I found myself reading the Bible with a new understanding and praying with a new relationship to Jesus. In the middle of the night, I suddenly woke up and found myself speaking very loudly in a new language. The effect on my personality too was immediate. The children all noticed it and said: "What on earth has happened to Dud?" (Which is what they call me: d-u-d.)

Faith: My experience was more gradual. I had to come to terms with tongues and realize that any gift from God was a joy, not a nuisance. When one night I did finally ask for the gift of tongues, I received it. One incident in particular convinced me that I was filled with the Spirit. For months, I had regularly been visiting a friend of mine, trying to lead her to the Lord. That night, as I repeated the very things I'd been telling her for months, she was converted and filled with the Spirit.

Tom: From that moment, God used our house to heal, change, and deliver. He showed us a new dimension of loving deeper: more vulnerable, completely open, not judging in any way, forgiving and therefore healing.

Faith: Our first experience of this involved a woman who had just lost one of her eyes. Tom has only got one eye so we identified immediately and invited her to come home with us. As she came to the Lord and was filled with the Spirit, she began to get better: the eyesight in her "good" eye (she couldn't see across the room or read without a magnifying glass) was completely restored. Spiritually, however, she became more and more peculiar, wandering off from time to time and growing extremely dependent on me.

Tom: The situation worsened until finally we called her doctor and discovered that the loss of her eye was a self-inflicted injury—not a result of cancer, as she had told us. "She won't respond to psychiatric treatment," the doctor said. "Even if she saw someone every day for the rest of her life, I doubt that she would be healed." We laughed; we couldn't think of anything else to do.

Faith: Meanwhile, however, we had learned about deliverance from the power of Satan. So one day, after this woman had deliberately spilled boiling water all over herself, Tom just said, "In the name of Jesus Christ, get out any of you there," and she was completely delivered. It wasn't instantaneous. She had an extraordinary background: her grandmother was a white witch; she'd been used as a medium, she'd had a curse put on her, and all sorts of things had to come out. But gradually, a complete and utter transformation took place. She's now a happily married woman, running a perfectly stable home.

Tom: As we saw more of the healing power of God, we grew anxious to move in the dimension of the Holy Spirit. A small prayer group had begun to form around the house, and when Faith and I took in a Pentecostal minister from the United States for a three-week rest, we invited her to speak to us. So Jean Darnall came and spoke, and afterwards several people were healed of physical sickness. It was an explosive time: the next week, 60 people came instead of 40; by the end of eight weeks, our numbers had increased to 350.

Despite encouragement, we were somewhat reluctant to continue these meetings. We didn't want this work to be a tower of Babel, something done from a fleshly point of view. After praying about it though, we did decide to go ahead and present a series of teachings on "the full purpose of the Kingdom of God." We prepared the course, still worried that we were doing it out of our own desires, but Faith received a word from the Lord that set our minds at rest.

Faith: On the morning that we were going to announce the course, I woke up with the syllables *ray-moth-gilly-add* going through my mind. After a bit, I thought, "Well, I'll go crazy if I keep thinking *ray-moth-gilly-add*," so I dismissed it altogether. Later as I was praying, the phrase came back to me so strongly that I determined to do all I could to find out what it meant. Finally, I checked the concordance and discovered that Ramoth Gilead was the first city of refuge that Moses had set up in the wilderness. This really corresponded to the way that God had used our house as a house of refuge. It showed us, too, that as we continued to open it up, God would build a city of refuge in and around our home.

Tom: We saw the beginnings of this in 1969 when Elmer Darnall, Jean's husband, joined us. Realizing our need for more solidly based teaching, he set up a Bible college which currently has an enrollment of 130 students. It aims at training effective Christian workers, especially encouraging those with strong leadership qualities into some form of charismatic service.

Most of our work has been oriented toward providing teaching for leaders. Rather than having large evangelistic meetings for the sake of evangelism, our purpose has been to encourage other people to be evangelists themselves. We've done this mainly by developing a tape ministry, by giving leaders' training conferences in different parts of the country, and by holding conferences and teaching meetings here at our home.

In 1970 we just burst out of the house into the garden, where we put up a tent with a seating capacity of 500. During 1972, between nine and ten thousand people came through the gates of the house to attend our conferences and teaching meetings.

Faith: More recently, after our tent blew away in a little private hurricane, a local vicar invited us to hold future conferences in his church. Since then we've been called to conduct renewal weekends in parishes all over the country, and this has become a significant part of our work.

Tom: Fortunately, the number of workers has kept pace with the fast growth of the outreaches. About 12 people, including four ordained ministers, have moved into the area to help us with the work. And over 50 people are involved in a support ministry of prayer and counseling, with a special concern for conference participants. We feel that we are being called as a team into a deeper commitment to one another and a sort of community relationship with one another, and we're now trying to understand the implications of this.

We have already seen how our commitment to the Lord has strengthened relationships within our own family. I am no longer overly possessive of my wife and have learned to trust the Lord in her. This hasn't always been easy, but the result has been a deeper love than ever before, a much more mature love.

Faith: As far as the children go, our relationship with them improved the moment we really committed them to the Lord. All our insistence on Jesus was only driving them farther away from him, so we relinquished them and stopped trying. Within months, they were all converted and filled with the Spirit.

Tom: Past experience has certainly taught us to trust the Lord for everything. We look forward to seeing more and more of his mighty works.

Faith: There's always more to learn; there's always more to give; there's always much more to be given.

Christian Hospitality

By Kevin Perrotta

Hospitality has always been an important source of life for God's Kingdom. Most of the Apostles traveled constantly, staying in the homes of people generous enough to receive them and trustworthy enough to serve them well. This is how Jesus instructed the Apostles to announce the coming of the kingdom, and it is how he himself lived. Because Jesus was poor, he was a guest in the homes of the people he preached to. In a town in Samaria, in the home of Martha and Mary, in Zaccheus' house, in the houses of Pharisees and tax collectors, Jesus called people to repentance, offered his forgiveness, and invited them into the Father's kingdom. He wanted to come among people as a guest and to use each visit to draw people to himself and to the Father.

In our home and our community, God has worked through hospitality in many ways. Many guests come to learn about Christian community; others come for personal reasons. A religious brother, on leave of absence from his own community, found healing and strength in the daily brotherly encouragement and admonition among the men he stayed with. A recently converted young man, who hadn't had much Christian fellowship or much time to pray, learned some basic truths about living for the Lord in the course of a two-week visit. A nun came for a week to make part of her annual retreat. She spent her time praying and reading Scripture, sharing with the women she lived with.

A Witness

We never know why the Lord has brought someone to us—there is no one answer or pattern. St. Paul tells the Romans that he expects there will be mutual encouragement in his visit with them. Often our guests inspire us. The deep faith and peace of many who stay with us remind us of the beauty and depth of what the Lord wants to do in us. Hearing about what he is doing in their lives increases our faith and our desire to look to him for all he wishes to accomplish.

Last summer, several of us were vacationing in Canada, close enough to drive to Sunday Mass at Madonna House, a lay apostolic community in rural, northern Ontario. We stayed after Mass and met many members of the community, who showed us their farm and explained a little about how the Lord was working among them. After dinner, as we were saying good-bye, my wife began to cry. "I wish we could stay," she said. "I feel like I'm leaving home." People had been generous and kind all afternoon; their love was a sign that, although we had not previously met, we were already part of one another, part of one family.

All our hospitality should be like this: a sign of our unity in the Lord.

In St. Paul's letters we can see how the early

Christians, practicing hospitality, were a source of joy and strength for one another. *"I was very happy,"* he wrote to the Corinthians, *"at the arrival of Stephanas, Fortunatus, and Achaicus, because they made up for your absence. They have refreshed my spirit as they did yours"* (1 Cor. 16:17-18). Hospitality is an opportunity to share our life in Christ. When we welcome others into the joy of our life together and share our food and our homes, we give them God's love. We can refresh one another, because the life we share is the life of Jesus.

Some months ago, when a woman named Peg arrived in Ann Arbor to visit our community, I took her to the apartment where she was to stay with about a half dozen women. Peg and I walked into the living room, and the women of the house, surprised in the middle of their daily routine, came to greet us. Peg gave a little exclamation, "Oh," she said, "it's so peaceful here." The peace and cheerfulness of that home seemed to lift Peg's fatigue from traveling. It also seemed to lift a deeper interior fatigue.

We can also proclaim God's glory by letting others see the ways he shapes our lives. Welcoming unbelievers into our home can be a powerful way to lead them to the Lord. Some people, even after meeting Christians and seeing changes in their lives, even talking about God and coming to prayer meetings, are unconvinced and unmoved. But even a short stay in a home where there is genuine love and affection and peace in people's ordinary lives, can affect skeptics in a powerful way. This is how I became a Christian. I had stopped in Ann Arbor on a visit and stayed as a guest. I was able to have faith in God because I was surrounded by people who constantly showed they had faith in him and loved him.

God wants to do much more through our hospitality than help people take their first steps toward him. He wants to deepen his love in our hearts and in our daily lives so that he can teach, encourage, and heal all who come into our homes. We need to ask him to show us how we can be of service to each person, friend or stranger, who comes into our home. We must consider each person important, and consider important the days or weeks that he lives with us.

Practical Ways

These are some practical considerations in serving our guests.

First, we should be united in our service. As a family or as a household, we need to pray and talk together about how we can best serve guests. We should decide how we can best use our facilities and time. Before a guest arrives, the family or household should agree on how we will spend time with him, and how its daily activities need to be changed to accommodate him. Although each person in the house will have something different to offer, each should feel that it is his personal responsibility to care for every guest.

Hospitality is sharing of our life together, and each person needs to share the life of the Lord among us. Even children, if they are taught how, can be sensitive to guests and can serve them in small but important ways. The father or whoever is head of the house has a responsibility of bringing the house together to serve guests, that all may grow in this service.

Second, we should begin each guest's visit in the

right way. A warm, affectionate welcome can put people at ease to receive what the Lord has for them. We should do whatever we can to make guests feel at home, and that they can rely on our love for them.

The head of the house should find out why a person has come to visit, what is particularly on his mind at this time, what he wants to do, what he wants to learn about. Even with friends and relatives, it is a good idea simply to ask someone why he has come, so that we can know how to serve him best. Perhaps a guest needs encouragement or counsel about a decision he has to make but he hesitates to tell us what is really on his heart. It is important just to ask. Unless we help him overcome his reticence, he may go away without receiving what he hoped to receive through his visit with us. Three young men once visited our community and, after they had been around for a few days, finally met someone who asked them why they had come. They said they had hoped that people in the community would pray with them to be baptized in the Holy Spirit. God might have been able to do much more if, when they first arrived, someone had found out why they had come.

Soon after a guest arrives, the head of the house or someone he chooses should help him plan his time. In order to help a person feel at home and participate in our life, we need to tell him about our routine: when we pray, when we eat and sleep, when the children go to bed, when we are usually all out of the house, and so forth. We need to coordinate what our guest will be doing with what will be going on in the house, and to arrange for the guest to do things and meet other people. Sometimes it is good to discuss a person's stay with him in detail.

Third, we should expect the Lord to bless our guests through their time with us, and to bless us through them. Therefore we should take care, not only of the physical needs of our guests, but also of their need to know God's love. Taking time to pray and talk together is one way of doing this. Often our guests will wait for us to suggest that they pray; we should eagerly take the initiative in this. Sharing the ways that we see God working in our lives day by day can help non-Christians come to faith in the Lord, and can strengthen and refresh those who already know him. Letting our guests meet others in our prayer group or community can give them a wider perspective on what God is doing among us.

We should help our Christian guests have time alone with God each day. Away from home, away from normal routine, it is easy to get so busy with new things that there is no time left for private prayer. Nevertheless, God wants to be at the center of our lives wherever we are; we should take time to praise him and listen to him each day. As hosts, we should help our guests have the discipline and order necessary to take time for prayer alone. They will feel free to take time for private prayer if they know we want them to, and they may need our help to see when they can do it. We often advise our guests to take the morning for prayer and reading, and to leave other things until afternoon and evening.

A Caution

Sometimes we undertake too much. For instance, because we want to see the Lord work in someone's life, we take him into our home, so that he can share in the love the Lord is giving us. This can be a wise and generous thing through which the Lord acts powerfully, but it can be foolish if we do not have the solidity in our relationship with Jesus and with one another to stand firm and overcome the problems. We need to be sober in our judgment of what we are able to do. When we follow the Lord we bear fruit; when we run ahead of him, we are confused and powerless.

Another limitation is the guest's willingness to receive what we can offer in the Lord and the Christian life. It is a legitimate service to give someone a place to stay who is not concerned about God but who needs lodging temporarily; often this is a sign to him of the Lord's love. Sometimes, however, a person tries to use our hospitality as a means of continuing to lead an un-Christian life. Though he may need a place to live, and show signs of turning to God, he should not take advantage of our hospitality to continue in wrongdoing. We need to discern whether the person is turning to the Lord or is delaying finding work and a place to live. If he is wrongly taking advantage of our hospitality he ought to leave.

It doesn't do a guest any good to be sheltered in irresponsibility and wrongdoing. We should tell him about his responsibility to provide for himself and exhort him to turn away from wrongdoing. Then we need to act on our words, taking care of the situation at once.

We all have much to learn in serving our guests. The Lord will be·with us to teach us step by step. We should be confident in him in serving our guests, and above all, we should be joyful and generous.

There is no limit to the blessings God can send you—he will make sure that you will always have all you need for yourselves in every possible circumstance, and still have something left over for all sorts of good works . . . For doing this holy service is not only supplying all the needs of the saints, but it is also increasing the amount of thanksgiving that God receives. By offering this service, you show them what you are, and that makes them give glory to God for the way you accept and profess the Gospel of Christ, and for your sympathetic generosity to them and to all (2 Cor. 9:8, 12-13).

Make Disciples
of all Nations

By Louise Bourassa

On an isolated Indian reserve in Manitoba, Canada, 50 or 60 people are gathered in a run-down log cabin. Outside, small groups of Indians crowd around the open windows to listen as a white man speaks.

Maynard Howe, missionary to the Cree and Saultex Indians, is preaching the Good News of Jesus Christ. "When you stand to preach," he observes, "the air is heavy, perspiration rolls; children play, crawling over your feet; babies cry; kids fight; dogs bark and sometimes fight under the house; mosquitoes chew at your neck and ankles; you preach by the light of a dim coal-oil lamp, a slow interpreter stammering dryly through your message. Your flesh feels like going home."

Home for the Howe family is St. Paul, Minnesota, but Maynard is by now almost as familiar with the Canadian wilderness, where he spends six to ten months a year. Working out of Calvary Bible Church, an independent fellowship in St. Paul, the 66-year-old evangelist has just completed his sixteenth rigorous year of bringing the Gospel to the Indians of northern Manitoba. "Don't feel sorry for me though," he grins. "It's an exciting life."

Adventure and excitement are to a certain extent inevitable in a territory as large and as rugged as Manitoba. Covering an area roughly the size of Texas, it falls into two geographical sections; the rolling plains of the south, and the rocky, sometimes thickly wooded region of the northern two-thirds. Because most Manitobans live in cities and towns (over half the total population is concentrated in the capital city of Winnipeg), much of this northern section is sparsely settled.

One of these isolated areas, the trackless wilderness north and east of 300-mile-long Lake Winnipeg, is Maynard's main sphere of activity. Scattered on remote reserves throughout the region are approximately 20,000 Indians who have had little or no contact with the Gospel. "I'm in an area where there are no roads," he explains. "I work out of 19 different reserves, the smallest of which is about 300 people, the largest, about 3,000. The reserves may be anywhere from 50 to 300 miles apart, and there's no connection between them other than by water or by air."

These factors affect transportation. Either alone, with his wife, or with a team, Maynard sets out by truck, often with a load of used clothing for the Indians; when the road ends, he continues by boat or by plane. Air travel is on government mail planes, fish planes, or freight planes, which land on the water either with pontoons or (after the winter freeze) with skis.

Up until eight years ago, travel by water meant cruising up and down the east shore of Lake Winnipeg in the Gospel boat, "Morning Star," and pitching a tent for outdoor meetings at each reserve. In 1966, however, the "Morning Star" was abandoned for the canoe in an effort to journey farther north than had previously been possible. Difficult portages over seldom-used trails, beaver dams, dangerous white rapids—a whole new set of challenges arose, but with them, too, a growing adaptability. "I go in," says Maynard, "with a pack on my back, a sleeping bag and a rolled-up foam rubber mattress, the minimum amount of cooking utensils, and my Bible. I may have to sleep under a tree, or maybe in a fish shack or vacant cabin."

Underlying this simple approach is a genuine love and respect for the Indians and their way of life: "If they sleep on the floor, I do. If they eat beaver, I do. I feel one with them and they with me. One of the biggest mistakes missionaries can make is to build a big church building, a big parsonage, put a fence around it and then live separate from the people, live aloof from them. The Indians are sensitive to that."

Despite this openness, however, hostility is the usual initial reaction to Maynard's arrival on a new reserve. Given the poverty, the violence, the substandard housing and education that figure in the lives of most of these Indians, their distrust of the white man is understandable and all too well-founded. "They figure you're after something," remarks Maynard. "So I try to tell them I'm not after something, I'm here to give them something."

What he gives them is the Good News of salvation. What the Lord gives them is first of all an assurance that this message is true. "Jesus will prove to you that he rose from the dead and is alive."

Maynard tells the Indians. "The Lord will prove to you that this is the true Gospel, and he will confirm it with signs following." Using Mark 16:17-20 as his guide, he then lays hands on those who are sick, expecting God to heal and thereby confirm his Word. And miracles happen. People are healed. Consequently, they believe, they repent, they turn to the Lord.

The following excerpts from Maynard's 1964 and 1967 reports present a vivid picture of such events.

"That night the tent was full, over two hundred were inside and just as many were outside. The very first night, nine Indians came down to repent and believe in Jesus Christ as their Savior. One Indian lady was healed of back trouble and instantly straightened up with a surprised look on her face. An Indian man with bad knees began to leap up and down. One man said he wanted to quit chewing snuff and we prayed for him. Two days later he came and testified that he had no desire for it anymore and had chewed for 25 years. Also healed was one lady who had such badly inflamed eyes that she could hardly sleep. She walked home through five miles of mud, mosquitoes, and slippery rocks and roots to babysit for her daughter so she could come and hear the Good News too. . . . A young boy, 12 years old, with a dumb spirit was brought in, and in Jesus' mighty name the Spirit was cast out. Before we left he was singing hymns in a clear, beautiful voice and was baptized in water and the Spirit.

"On August fifth, seven more desired water baptism, and while about three hundred or more Indians lined the bank, the power of God again fell and 17 more were baptized in water. The scene was repeated as almost everyone was baptized in the Holy Spirit. Many young men and women were so drunk in the Holy Spirit they could hardly stand. They wept, danced, leaped, clapped their hands, spoke in tongues, shouted.

"Next night we were at the other end of the reserve in an Indian chapel. Again, several danced before the Lord; one elderly woman, one of the elders, and several young people praising Jesus in the dance."

Himself amazed at each new demonstration of God's love and power, Maynard is nonetheless not surprised. He insists that if we preach the Gospel like the apostles did, "telling people to repent and make a full surrender to the Lord Jesus Christ," then God is under obligation to confirm it. "This is one way the Lord advertises his wonderful love for us," he adds.

For all their awesomeness, however, these signs and wonders are pointless without their desired effect: "the greatest miracle of all, the conversion of a person from his old, sinful ways." Once this miracle takes place and an Indian is intent on following Jesus, he is baptized in water. This is usually also the moment the Lord chooses to baptize him in the Holy Spirit. Maynard writes: "Most all the Indians are filled with the Holy Spirit right there in the water, some through the laying on of hands, some just automatically. We don't tell them anything about tongues, but about 80-85 percent of them usually come out of the water speaking in tongues and prophesying."

As a follow-up to this initial experience, Maynard remains on the reserve for several weeks. Often working with John Golas, a Ukrainian farmer and convert from one of the earlier tent meetings, and Kenny Anderson, a Minnesota florist, he teaches and encourages the new Christians. Later, when some of the Indians have matured in the Life in the Spirit and meet the criteria set forth in I Timothy 3, elders (leaders) are appointed to continue the work once the team has moved on to another reserve.

From time to time, according to requests for help or to the promptings of the Holy Spirit, the team returns. Sometimes they help build a chapel when the Christians have become too numerous to meet in private homes; sometimes they present more extensive teaching; sometimes they attend fellowship meetings involving Indians from several different reserves. Always, they encourage their new brothers and sisters to hold fast to the truth.

No Indian Christian will find this easy. On the reserve, persecution—whether from hardened sinners, from adherents to the old Indian religion, or from "religious" people who don't know the love of Jesus—is a reality. More often than not, the "shakers," as they are derisively called, face insults, beatings, unemployment. "Occasionally," Maynard reports, "they find a big rock put through the bottom of their canoe, or come home and find their windows all knocked out of the log cabin. One storekeeper even refused to sell groceries to the Christians."

Maynard's own personal catalogue of perils and near mishaps reads like a modern-day account of St.

Paul: "Well, I nearly lost my life three times in storms, once was nearly 'brained' by a demon-possessed native woman wielding a home-made oak chair, once was beaten by some drunken men on a reserve and often in peril as we negotiated raging rapids, struck submerged rocks, or weathered storms." Nor had he escaped direct persecution. Beaten once by order of the local witch doctor, Maynard has long been a target of criticism by denominational missionaries, who see him as an invader to their territory.

All this, however, is changing, as the fruit of his work becomes evident in the transformed lives of the converts. "There's still persecution," Maynard comments, "but not like there used to be." Now, with the charismatic renewal as a common denominator, he is finding it possible to work with various missionaries. Joyfully, he recalls a recent conversation with an elderly Catholic priest, who, stationed for years on an isolated reserve, knew nothing of the charismatic renewal until Maynard's visit and gift of several issues of *New Covenant*. "I've been praying for this for a long time," responded the priest with tears in his eyes.

Despite the tapes, tracts, and correspondence that he attends to whenever he is at home in Minnesota, Maynard has also found the time and energy to preach in Guatemala, British Honduras, Saskatchewan, and the Yukon. Now, as Indian preachers carry on the work of evangelizing their own people, he is travelling more among charismatic prayer groups in the United States. He finds this as exciting as preaching in the Manitoban wilderness, because he sees the renewal as a unifying factor among all Christians: "God is surely doing a strange work in the earth today—Baptists, Anglicans, Methodists, Catholics, Apostolics, Presbyterians, and Pentecostals—all meeting together, worshipping Jesus and sharing his word and his works together."

Praying with his wife for directions in this new venture, Maynard is quick to glorify God in advance for any good that may come out of his involvement. Of the signs and wonders he has seen and will see he says, "God does it all."

To illustrate the point he fondly recounts this story about his first exhilarating experience of preaching in the bush country:

> *"I came back and I was telling my wife about the wonderful things that had happened up there. She looked at me and evidently saw some pride there and said, 'Well, that's wonderful, honey, to hear what the Lord did, but you want to remember that he used a donkey in the Old Testament.'*
>
> *That winter I went back up there and several people told me about Grandma Jewett. 'Before we became Christians,' they said, 'we'd sneak up and look in her window and she'd be laying on her face, crying and speaking some kind of strange language. Then, we didn't know what was the matter with her. Now we know.'*
>
> *Well, I met Grandma Jewett and I found out that this gray-haired widow woman had prayed for nine solid years for that community."*

The story's conclusion and Maynard's summary of his sixteen years in Manitoba: "All *I* did was go up there and pick some ripe plums."

Bearing the
Word of the Lord

By Maynard Howe

I was born in 1909 on a Minnesota farm. My family was not Christian and we never went to church.

I first became aware of the Lord about 32 years ago, when my wife found Jesus Christ in a little prayer meeting. She didn't say very much except that she knew Jesus as her personal savior, but she was so different that it seemed to me I had a new wife.

I wanted to be like her, but I was very proud and very busy doing other things. I was a business-man at the time, in advertising and printing, and belonged to several lodges and business associations. I sought out excitement in hunting and fishing, and in teaching judo and karate. I knew that if I gave my heart to the Lord, many of my idols would go by the wayside. So I hung on and fought, resisting the Gos-pel in every possible way.

As the months went on, everything that I touched went wrong and I saw that God was dealing with me. One night in a prayer meeting (I still don't know how I got there) I heard a young man preach the Word of God. At first I thought that maybe my wife had told him about me: he was talking about everything that was wrong in my life. But I realized that the Lord was speaking to me. I saw that I had never really surrendered to the Lord Jesus Christ, and so I got down on my knees and asked him to change my life. Instantly something happened in me, something happened in my inner man.

From that time on, things were different. Gambling, smoking, drinking, swearing—those things disappeared, and I had no more desire for them. I found that some of the lodges and clubs I belonged to were doing things that I couldn't do as a Christian, and so I dropped my membership. The Lord began to deal with me about being honest, and I had to straighten up some of my business practices.

We began going to an evangelical church where the pastor would take a book out of the Bible and preach a whole chapter every Sunday. We went through the book of Luke that way, and then one morning he said, "Now, we're going to study the most dangerous book in the Bible." And he opened up to the book of Acts. Now this particular church did not believe in prophecy or in speaking in tongues; they did not believe in laying on hands for the healing of the sick or in casting out devils. All that, they said, had passed away with the apostles.

When we got to the eighth chapter of Acts where Philip heals the sick and casts out devils, where Peter and John pray for people and lay hands on them for the baptism in the Holy Spirit, I started wondering. I began to see that a person could be converted to Jesus Christ, yet not have received power for witnessing and serving the Lord.

Meanwhile, something happened to make me

think. Our second oldest daughter, a young baby at the time, had cardiac asthma. Even though we moved out to the country so she could benefit from the fresh air, the doctor said that she would probably not live. My wife and I were quite despondent about this, but one day we came across Mark 16:17-18: *"And these signs will accompany those who believe . . . they will lay their hands on the sick and they will recover."* We went back to the pastor with it and he said we could pray, but without laying hands on. The whole church did pray, but nothing happened.

Finally, one night, we went into our little girl's room, got down on our knees, put our hands through the crib and laid them upon her. We believed and we prayed and asked the Lord to heal her. He did: our daughter is now married and the mother of four lovely children. No more cardiac asthma.

Naturally, after this we were convinced that we ought to be filled with the Holy Spirit. Again I went to the pastor. "Brother," he said, "you can ask the Lord, but just stay away from the holy rollers."

"Pastor," I said, "who are the holy rollers?"

"I don't know any of 'em right now, but they roll on the floor and they climb the walls and swing on the chandeliers."

I promised him I wouldn't go near anyone like that, and I began to seek the Lord in my room all by myself. This was 25 years ago, when no one except the Pentecostals had ever heard of being baptized in the Holy Spirit. There were no Pentecostal people in our neighborhood, and there was no charismatic movement. We had never heard of a Lutheran or a Baptist or a Methodist or a Presbyterian ever receiving the baptism in the Holy Spirit.

But one evening as I was praying, I had a tremendous meeting with the Lord Jesus Christ. My body was saturated with the love and the fire and the power of God, so that I could hardly contain it. I was full of joy, full of love. It felt like fire was going through me and my bones seemed full of rejoicing.

I had been reading the book of Acts, and I felt that I should also speak in tongues. It didn't dawn on me until two nights later, however, that the tremendous experience I'd had before was the baptism in the Holy Spirit. I began to thank the Lord, and as I did so, I spoke in another language—in tongues.

The pastor didn't say much when I told him, but he started asking me to take over the services whenever he was away. People began coming to me with questions: "Brother Howe, what's happened to you? You pray different and you preach different, and something has happened to you. Could you tell us what it is?" And I would tell them about my experience.

Shortly afterwards, my wife and three of our children were baptized in the Holy Spirit. It wasn't long before reports about other people were circulating. One sister began to speak in tongues right in the middle of ironing clothes. A deacon got to work two hours late one morning because he was baptized in the Holy Spirit while driving to his job. My Sunday school class of teenagers started asking questions, and pretty soon about half of them were filled with the Spirit.

We began to have prayer meetings in our home, and sometimes on those Saturday nights we'd have as many as 70 and 80 people from various denominations. As the Lord led us, we laid hands on some of them for the baptism in the Holy Spirit. We prayed for the sick and for those who needed deliverance from evil spirits. Our lives became so noticeably charged with the Spirit of God that our numbers grew and finally, about a third of the church was filled with the Spirit.

Of course in the church itself we didn't speak in tongues or prophesy or do anything that the pastor didn't agree with. Eventually though, we got a new minister: one who was violently opposed to the outpouring of the Holy Spirit. Sunday mornings, he would tell us why tongues are not for us today; Sunday evenings, the message was why healing is not for us today. It was hard to sit there and listen, but we didn't know what else to do. We stayed as long as we possibly could, but when our children started getting confused, I resigned as deacon and Sunday school teacher. We started meeting and worshipping with the other families that had been forced out of the church.

One day as I was praying and reading in the book of Deuteronomy, one verse impressed me so that I couldn't let go of it: *"You have been going about this mountain country long enough; turn northward."* I really didn't know what the Lord meant, but the more I prayed about it the more I knew that God was somehow turning my head to the north. Now I didn't know anybody up there except one young preacher in northern Minnesota. Maybe the Lord wanted me to go up and help him out. Twice I took a leave of absence from my job and worked back in the bush country with this preacher. And God did a wonderful thing there: about 60 people gave their lives to the Lord, and almost every one was filled with the Holy Spirit.

I returned home, still unsure about what to do. Several months later, a stranger stood up in our Sunday service and said that he had felt impelled to come up from Florida. Suddenly he started to prophesy to me: "You've gone north, but you haven't gone far enough. God has called you to go preach the Gospel to a dark-skinned people. He will fill them with the Spirit. He will heal their sick bodies. He will supply all of your needs. The Lord will take care of your children." And then he quoted the verse from Deuteronomy: the same verse that the Lord had given me. I began to pray about this in earnest.

Soon after, I was asked to preach the Gospel in southern Manitoba. Another brother and I went and found a group of French people who were inquiring about the way of salvation. After one of our services there, a man I didn't know said to me: "You should take this Gospel farther north." And he told me about the many Indian people on the reserves.

When I came back home I was still praying and still undecided. Full-time missionary work was a big step for a father of eight children. Again the Lord guided me, this time through a missionary from India—again someone I didn't know. "The Lord is going to take care of your children," he said to me. "He is going to take care of their education." That decided me. Sixteen years have passed since then, and I have seen God fulfill every promise.

We've never had to ask anyone for money, and the Lord has provided abundantly for the education of all the children. My oldest boy is now a certified public accountant; my oldest daughter is a registered nurse; the second girl became an X-ray technician; my second oldest boy got his Ph.D. from Kent University and the next boy will be a chiropractor after one more year of study; the other boy is working and has his masters from Rochester Tech; the next girl is a teacher with a B.A. from the University of Minnesota; the youngest boy is still in college. More important, all of our children are filled with the Spirit, as are the spouses of the six married ones, and as are most of our grandchildren.

Before I knew the Lord, I used to ask my Christian friends what they did for excitement. "Well, we just love Jesus," they would say. I thought they were just a bunch of sissies, but now I know what they meant. These 16 years of working on Indian reserves have been the best time of my life.

Loving Jesus is really exciting!

"Gray Hairs Are a Glorious Crown"

By James D. Manney

Man has always regarded old age ambivalently. The "glorious crown" of Proverbs has its modern counterpart in our "golden years" and "senior citizens." God made respect for old age an important part of the law: *honor thy father and mother.* Over the centuries, Jewish rabbis have taught a consistent attitude toward age: God confers old age on the righteous.

Yet the Psalmist's lament suggests an ugly reality behind the ideal. The Law demanded respect for the Hebrew elders, but the people often ignored them instead. The Psalmist expresses an eternal fear: the old man's fear of personal weakness and abandonment by his people; the young man's fear of his father's fate, the time when he will no longer be a man.

Today, one of every 10 Americans is aged 65 or over. The percentage is even higher in most Western European countries, and everywhere the numbers and percentage of older people are rising.

Older people generally live apart: in their own homes and apartments, in special retirement colonies, in dreary flats in deteriorating central cities, in nursing homes, homes for the aged; on geriatric wards of mental hospitals. For all their large numbers—21 million in the United States—older people are surprisingly invisible. We do not see them on the streets, in theaters and restaurants, in stores and other public places. Except for a few highly respected judges, politicians, theologians, and writers, older people have no visibility at all in social, economic, political, or religious life.

Further, a third of all the poor people in the United States are aged 65 or over, nearly a quarter of all older Americans live in officially defined poverty, and millions more live in the twilight zone just above the official poverty line. In most Western European countries, older people are the largest group of the poor. Since most older people live on Social Security, pensions, and other fixed incomes, most must fight an anxious struggle against inflation. An income which is adequate at the time of retirement is destined to become less and less adequate as time goes on. Thus, most old people become relatively poorer as they grow older.

Besides poverty, other familiar social problems are magnified for older people. A third of all older Americans live in substandard housing. Perhaps a third of the older people living in the community have serious need for mental health care. Americans aged 65 and over constitute the most malnourished segment of the population. Older people who happen to be black, Spanish-speaking, Oriental, Indian, rural residents, or widows are also poorer, sicker, and more isolated than any other groups in the American population.

Why is this so? It is hard to avoid the conclu-

sion that the attitudes of younger people, along with
the values of society as a whole, largely create and
sustain the social problem of aging. I first suspected
this when I spoke with a young minister, just out of
seminary, about his first experiences in a church. He
told me that he was shocked and disappointed to
find that about half of the congregation was composed, of old people. "I was fired up for the youth
ministry," he said, "but there weren't any young
people around, just these middle class families and
the aged. I didn't know what to say when an old
woman came to tell me privately that she suspected
her children were plotting to send her to a nursing
home."

"That was my first real life counseling session. I
thought that the big problem was to alleviate the
children's guilt at having to send their mother away.
I did that with minimal success, I think. But I never
really considered the old woman's needs and fears. I
assumed that she was really sick and had to accept
the inevitable with a minimum of anguish for
everyone else. In retrospect, I think I blew it."

There are other examples of modern attitudes
toward old people. In a small city near Ann Arbor,
an old woman wandered away from a nursing home
not long ago. It was 12 hours before the woman's
frantic daughter was able to convince the sheriff's
department to send out a search party. I have heard
social agency administrators, social workers, doctors, psychiatrists, and other service people say that
they deliberately avoid old people because they
would rather spend their time and resources on more
"promising" cases.

This attitude toward old people is both tragic

and ironic. It is tragic because the negative, depressing, hopeless view of aging is largely a self-fulfilling prophecy. Since aging is a gradual and differential process, older people learn that they are "old" through the reactions and cues of the people around them. Thus, the attitudes of younger people deeply influence the way their elders live their lives.

The irony of the situation is that advances in medical science and increasing economic affluence are making the negative view of aging less and less tenable. For the first time in history, large numbers of people are healthy enough to live many vigorous years beyond age 65. Societies are becoming wealthy enough to support them. Yet the options open to older people steadily narrow. Compulsory retirement is becoming the norm, and retirement is occurring at ever earlier ages. Retirement from work is often quickly followed by retirement from other situations, such as clubs, community groups, and church activities. The most frequent leisure activity for older people is watching television.

Christians who are concerned with older people and who wish to address the social problems involved with aging must begin by confronting personal and social attitudes toward age. We have been formed by a culture which holds that old age is bad and youth is good; that innovation, newness, and daring are better than tradition and experience; and that the physical decline of age cancels out other possible gains.

These attitudes are embedded in our actions, our words, and our patterns of thought. I recently realized how all-pervasive the negative view of aging is when I worked on a Life in the Spirit Seminar composed mainly of students from the University of Michigan. After talking to several of these students, I found my self regretting that I was 28 years old, a full decade beyond my own heady and hectic freshman year, and in some ways unable to communicate with these young men. Only later did I realize that I am often ill at ease with older people as well. But being unable to talk easily with old people was somehow less important than talking easily with young college students. The subconscious value—"youth is better"—rose automatically to the surface.

A serious misconception of aging lies beneath the myths and stereotypes. We in Western societies conceive of aging primarily as an irreversible, unmanageable process of biological decline. The very word "aging" conjures up biological images: gray hair, wrinkles, weakness, fatigue, stooping, shuffling walk, sickness, pain.

Other cultures and societies have not been so dour. The Chinese philosopher Confucius thought old age essential for clear thinking and the pursuit of truth. Plato's *Republic* is an extended dialogue into the components of a happy and wise old age. The leaders of the early Christian community were called "elders." They were older, mature men, chosen for their wisdom and for their tested ability to discern the leadings of the Spirit. A pattern emerges. Throughout history, men have experienced aging as a continued improvement of their capacities, as a continual discovery of their true selves. Today, this experience is a rare exception.

Today's radical movement toward Christian community must involve a radical return to this historical human experience of aging as a process of growth. God's work to transform the social order through the charismatic renewal must necessarily involve a transformation of the disheartening position of older people in modern society. Only a radical Christian fellowship, based on the person of Jesus Christ and led by his Holy Spirit, can fundamentally change the tenuous position of the retired man, the loneliness of the widow, the often masked depression of the older person who can no longer make a serious contribution to the life of his community.

Christian community is the long-range solution, but we must begin to change our own attitudes toward aging. We fear aging; we avoid older people. This attitude of avoidance and distaste is the main reason why older people are largely segregated from the rest of society, a separation which impoverishes the young as much as it alienates the old. The remedy begins on a purely individual level as we examine the process of our own aging, and as we reach out personally to those whose remaining days can be measured in months and years instead of decades.

One important way we can begin to change our hearts about aging is to watch our words. Our characteristic attitudes toward old people emerge quite clearly in our language. We scorn old people ("old coot," "old fool"); find them rigid and useless ("you can't teach an old dog new tricks"); think they are silly ("old biddy"); and find them physically repulsive ("dirty old man"). When I become an "older person," I hope these phrases will be just as embarrassing as racial expletives are today.

The charismatic prayer group constitutes a special difficulty. While the charismatic movement now represents a cross-section of the population, it is still dominated by the young and, to some extent, the middle-aged. Evening meetings and the grueling pace of charismatic life surely inhibit the participation of many older people. The emphasis in the charismatic renewal on innovation, newness, and change may also be uncongenial to many older people. After all, most have seen many renewal movements come and go, with high hopes giving way to modest accomplishments. Whatever the reason, older people, especially those with unmet social, physical, and psychological needs, seem underrepresented in the charismatic renewal as it exists today.

To remedy the situation, we need to reach out—with tact, sensitivity, and generosity of spirit. When asked what their churches could do to help them most, more than anything else, old people wanted more home visits from pastors and others. This is a valuable clue. Physically, many older people are partially disabled and cannot move around easily. Psychologically, they tend to avoid the rat race of meetings and projects and wish to spend more time in intimate, expressive relationships with friends. Socially, many fight a losing battle with the requirements of independent living. They need help with shopping and cooking, a willing hand to put up screens in the summer and storm windows in winter, a strong friend to mow the lawn and move furniture. Some gerontologists estimate that half the older people living in nursing homes, homes for the aged, and other institutions could live independently if they had adequate help with these chores.

Finally, Christians should take a concern for society's treatment of the elderly. Most communities do very little for their older citizens; nearly every social institution responds inadequately to their needs. There are many examples of this. While adult education programs in local schools have grown remarkably in the past 10 years, their administrators have made little effort to attract older people. Middle-aged and older people who want jobs experience serious discrimination in employment. Most public transportation systems are too dangerous and uncomfortable for frail older people to use. Public buildings and private homes are seldom designed for use by old people with limited mobility. While older people constitute more than 10 per cent of the population, they constitute only two per cent of the outpatients seen in community mental health centers. Many doctors, psychiatrists, nurses, social workers, and other professionals have an aversion to dealing with elderly people. The health conditions in hundreds of nursing homes are shocking, and state and federal efforts to enforce strict rules in these facilities are, for the most part, scandalously inadequate. The list goes on and on, touching everywhere, implicating everybody.

To sum up, a Christian approach to aging would include these three dimensions: (1) a change in our personal attitudes toward older people and toward our own aging; (2) work for a fuller recognition of older people's needs and potential contributions in our churches and prayer groups; and (3) an informed and resolute participation in efforts to ameliorate the social problems older people face. As Christians, we approach this challenge with an insight that our age-segregated, youth-worshipping society refuses to accept: that God works to bring all his people together and that the source of our unity is in knowledge of his son Jesus Christ. Thus, age has unshakable dignity, and the process of aging itself promises nothing less than a growing breadth and depth of our knowledge of our Savior.

Troubled Youths and a Household

By Bob Horning

Partly as a result of a visit by an American priest, Charles and Kasia Waldegrave and some friends began a ministry to the oppressed and criminal youth of Hamilton, New Zealand.

Charles Waldegrave became involved in the Christian faith while studying at Massey University in Palmerston North. There he joined others on the campus in an extensive ministry among their fellow students under the guidance of the chaplain. They began a large central charismatic prayer group for the purpose of teaching, worship and sharing. Through their witness they were able to penetrate many sub-cultural groups within the university. The numbers grew continually, even though students were leaving at the end of each year.

But Charles felt God wanted to use people who were involved in the charismatic movement for something deeper. In 1971 Graham Pulkingham of the Church of the Redeemer in Houston, Texas, came to New Zealand, and things began to fall in place for Charles, his wife Kasia, and some other students at Waikato University in Hamilton where they had moved for post-graduate study.

When Fr. Pulkingham talked about living together in a community and reaching out to others in need, 14 students knew that was what they wanted. They rented a house, and although they did not all live together, they committed themselves to each other in a covenant relationship. Their aim was to commit themselves to expressing in community and social action the more mystical side of their faith, to let the power of the Holy Spirit in their lives affect others. They would share their lives with those who missed security, love, and affection. They would build a family for oppressed people.

Charles went to court to offer to take an offender into their community instead of having him sent to jail or the detention center. And from that point on many different people came to live with them.

Some of these youths had committed violent crimes, some were Maoris (brown-skinned people native to New Zealand, of Polynesian origin) who found the transition to the city difficult; some had drug and alcohol problems; some were wives who would stay to avoid a beating at home; some had no home; some had psychiatric problems.

The number coming in was intentionally kept fewer than the core group so they could minister to them adequately. Later on, as quite a number of those who entered the house in need became core members, two more houses were set up.

The first nine months of this life were fruitful, but at the same time a difficult learning experience. The youths who were criminals didn't automatically change when they were brought into the house. They broke plates, stole clothes, scribbled on walls.

The Waldegraves were admittedly naive, but they didn't have any manuals or precedents to look to. They learned through experience.

As Kasia said, "Our main ministry was to offer love. God is love, so through love they saw God to the best of their ability and discernment. There is a temptation in Christian circles to think we will straighten people out, but it is God who does it through our love."

Alienation in society was the cause of most of the disorder in the young people, Charles felt, and this is what this household wanted to overcome. "In our cities we often don't talk to each other. We frequently don't know our next door neighbors. Seldom do we really share together, and most of us would be very loath to lend our car for a couple of weeks to a neighbour for hospital visiting, or even for a holiday, just two of many possible examples. These sorts of difficulties can lead to symptomatic problems in our society like drug abuse.

The core group knew possessions might get broken, dirtied or stolen, but they also knew they were being asked to commit "not some spooky part of our beings, but our cars, checkbooks, homes."

As a result of the experiences of this first nine months they agreed upon a workable set of minimal groundrules. These related to their commitment to one another, the sharing of tasks and financial needs, the building of community through recreation, and issues concerning sexual relations and the law.

It wasn't just a life of rules, however; it was a life of love and choice. Nobody was forced to become a Christian in order to live in the house. They were told upon entering the house that its foundation was Christian, but that they were not expected to participate in house bible-studies or sharing or prayer unless they wanted to. The core group wanted them to experience the love of the Christian body and to choose as they wished.

A dramatic example of change was Bill, who had spent much of his life in boy's training centres and borstal. His father had beaten him with bicycle chains as a child. He had committed serious crimes, and had even tried to kill himself. He was an angry young man when he came to the house. His wife was pregnant, and he used to drink dangerously to escape the tension within himself. Life in the house mellowed and freed him, enabling him after a year to live happily with his wife and baby. He stopped infringing the law and was later able to move out with his family into his own home.

Not every case in the house was a success, but most of the people responded to the love of the house, often without knowing what they were responding to. They knew they were loved and accepted, which was for some, something new. As such quite a number drifted into faith.

One person who was involved in crime before coming to the house, gave up his crime, paid off his debts, eventually became a member of the core group, and was made responsible for house finances.

Kasia and some others taught basic arithmetic, spelling and other subjects that were requested, since quite a number were barely literate. On Monday nights the core group would gather to talk and pray about household needs, how to make someone feel more at home, or talk about forthcoming court proceedings.

On Wednesday night there was an open Bible study, and the core group had to develop a question-answer type study since a number of the young people could not read very well.

The people coming in were also expected to contribute—either by working or going to school. Often the kids were refused employment because of their records, so Charles sometimes arranged interviews for them so the employers could see the kids were now in a stable home and more likely to work well.

Chores in the house were not apportioned, but were left to be done as anyone saw the need. This was another way of reinforcing that nobody was being coerced but were being left the choice to live lives of love and consideration.

The results of this type of life together were enormous on the household members and even the city of Hamilton. Deviant behaviour largely disappeared from those living in the house. This also rubbed off on others loosely associated with them.

The core group learned to interact with one another without having one person designated as boss. They learned to love and share with those of different cultural backbrounds. They learned what Christ's love calls for in helping people in difficult situations. They had to give up selfishness and give when people asked of them.. From the Maoris they learned innocence, the value of spontaneous music, how to better live communally.

Quite a number of citizens in Hamilton recognized the house as an example of racial harmony. Besides the Maoris and whites, there were a few people of other nationalities. As a result of seeing something that worked, many wanted to help. Doctors offered free treatment, lawyers offered free aid.

Charles has spoken about the principles of community and commitment to several men's and women's groups, to parish councils, and on retreats.

He had the chance to call Christians to commitment. He says, "We have a clever way of excusing ourselves from helping the needy of the world. The rich, in general, want quiet streets, sufficiently removed from the poor to be able to ignore their existence, so they don't have to speak to their neighbours or get involved in the city's problems. But helping these people is the responsibility and purpose of the church."

Working with Young People

By Pete Perona

Early this summer I met a fifteen-year-old boy named Ken at a park where our community was meeting for a picnic. He was drawn to our activity by the music and general commotion we generate as a young community. As we talked he mentioned that he had once been what he termed a "Jesus person," but that it did not work out for him due to a particular hang-up he had. He was not resentful or mocking, but genuinely disappointed in the Jesus he had tried to relate to. I could sense in him a deep longing for help, but also an air of guilt and hopelessness stemming from his failure to "make it" with God.

When I first experienced Christ loving me I was a senior in college and never imagined that anyone Ken's age was serious enough to turn to the Lord. I was so excited at the time about the Gospel that I longed to go into full-time Christian service, but automatically ruled out the possibility of working with teenagers. I wanted to affect people who were old enough to appreciate and appropriate the love and power of God. To be honest, I had little concern and even less hope for teenagers. Over the last seven years, however, God has instilled in me by the working of his Spirit all the love and hope needed to serve them.

The change began immediately after college during my one and only year of religious education when I chose as my service project the responsibility of teaming up with some of my friends to lead a high school Christian club. As I recall, I made this choice more for the sake of doing something with my friends than for the sake of working with high school people. The project involved a once-a-week visit to a home where five to fifteen teens at various levels of Christian experience met to pray, study the Bible, ask questions, and talk with their friends. I felt confident with younger people and important to them, but as time progressed I found the project to be a frustrating experience. Teenagers, as I initially suspected, appeared to lack the maturity necessary to experience a lasting effect from the Gospel. Their spiritual life was often like a cheap roller-coaster ride: exciting, lots of ups and downs, over quickly with little to no progress. Ken's initial interest and his subsequent fall were quite typical of those of his age.

Jesus clearly instructed his disciples that they should bear fruit and that their fruit should abide. I saw myself, however, and other Christian workers leading countless young people to the Lord with the unfortunate end result being that the majority drifted away. This experience left me with a growing sense of failure both to the teens and to the Lord. At the time it seemed impossible for most young people to mature in the Lord in light of their personalities, their environment, and the gross void of practical wisdom necessary to provide answers that would make Christianity work for them. My conviction grew to the point that I could no longer justify teen-age evangelism where neither I nor anyone I knew of could provide the care necessary for growth. Upon completion of my year of seminary I decided not to continue my ministry with high-school-age people.

For the next year, I concentrated mostly on my own spiritual growth and development as a Christian entering society. I still desired a ministry for Christ and prayed that if it was also God's desire he would prepare me for it. I began to notice, however, a growing sense of frustration with my own spiritual life. Slowly I found it harder to pray and read Scripture. Old sin patterns crept back into my life despite my determination to defeat them. Most important of all, I gradually lost my sense of personal warmth with the Lord. I would search the Scriptures desperately, read from others' experiences, and talk with older Christians in an attempt to find something to pray, to think, to do that could reverse the trend. Rededications only ended in greater frustration and loss of hope. I knew too much about Christ to deny the truth of the Gospel, but apparently too little about abiding in him to keep my light burning brightly. I slowly found myself settling for a lukewarm Christian life, and as I looked around the whole Church seemed to be drugged into the same state of ineffectiveness. Looking back I realized that my spiritual life was quite similar to that of the teenagers I had worked with. My roller-coaster ride, however, took longer; but that was because I was, like most adults, willing to put up with inconsistencies over a longer period of time without giving up and trying something new.

Hearing about the charismatic renewal and experiencing it gave me new hope. I saw long-dead Christians, young and old, come back to life with a lasting power, excitement, and hope. I, myself, found renewed life by being drawn closer to Christ than ever before by his love for me. I also experienced a greater expectation in my own potential for service to his kingdom. But the key element of lasting life and hope came for me from the experience of community life where brothers and sisters in the Lord strive together, upholding one another in sickness and in health. I quickly gained a new confidence in the Gospel and its power to bring not simply new, but lasting life and freedom to all, even teenagers!

Just after I came into the renewal, God led me to a small group of teenagers at a nearby church who had also been recently touched by the Spirit. We began to pray together regularly, and I saw God bless their youthful excitement and openness to his Spirit. Together we grew in our love for the Lord and for one another, experienced the various gifts and ministries of the Spirit, and watched the Lord adding other young people to our number. I could not help but wonder if we could weather the trials and discouragements sure to follow, but as they arose and we confronted them together we found a new strength as a growing body. God continually called us individually and collectively to present ourselves as a living sacrifice, not conformed to this world, but transformed by the renewal of our minds that we might show forth the will of God, proving it to be good and acceptable and perfect. It was not easy, for we had to face all the typical issues of our society as they affect teenagers. Dating, sexuality, authority, and roles of men and women were, and still are, the major areas of rethinking, dying to self, and growth.

As we struggled together we slowly saw the roller-coaster spiritualities level off as individuals experienced a gradual but continuous release from various forms of bondage and frustration. We discovered and put into effect God's life-bringing Word in areas which had previously been sources of guilt, fear, disappointment, despair, and self-condemnation. Family situations began to heal where bitterness and hate had existed. Personal relationships developed which produced fruits of acceptance, personal warmth, affection, openness, and freedom in sharing where there had been isolation, fear of rejection, jealousy, guilt, and shame. Understandings of self-image improved, yielding self-acceptance, hope, purpose, peace, joy, and thanks to God. We experienced personally that there really was nothing that could separate us from the love of Christ: no family situation, no sin problem, no past experience, no fleshly desire, no fear. We gained a new hope for ourselves and others that Christianity actually does work; and when it doesn't appear to, we can find out why and what to do about it. Having this assurance has been one of the most important blessings that God has bestowed on us, for it has freed us to expose our difficulties without fear of there not being a workable solution. In addition, the deep bonds of love and trust that have resulted from sincere and stable commitments to Christ and to one another have produced an atmosphere of openness and acceptance without fear of condemnation and rejection. In all, God has been making it increasingly possible for everyone to air before at least a few brothers and sisters all the common desires and fears that typically remain hidden inside and gradually poison the lives of young people who need to be real.

One of the most encouraging aspects of what I have seen developing over the three years we have been together is the growing ability of the teens to apply God's wisdom not simply to their own lives, but to others. Many high school Christian groups are seriously disabled in that counseling is given only by the "leader(s)". Overdependence on leaders and a lack of responsibility in personally seeking wisdom are the common pitfalls of individual teenagers, and groups. In an abundance of counselors, there is wisdom, and as teens begin to give instead of always receiving help, they discover new depths of understanding and fulfillment which foster the sense of personal worth necessary to all. We now have people in our core community from the ages of twelve to thirty, caring for one another in give-and-receive relationships whereby each is able to find love, personal warmth, support, guidance, and acceptance from people of both sexes without all the common fears and tensions that typify our society. God first directed and enabled us to build solid relationships with others of the same sex, and just over this past summer began to encourage and free us in relating to those of the opposite sex without the overpowering desire or fear of a possessive, exclusive relationship.

All this is not to say that we are without problems and failures. We continue to face personal and group obstacles which threaten us, and we must constantly be before the Lord for his promised help. There are still some who fall away, but they are the exception, not the rule, and often return at a later time. We make bad decisions and poor judgments, but we believe that God has geared his plan in accordance with our natural deficiencies, and we trust in his ability to more than make up for our imperfections. We have greatly benefited from the teaching, strength, and encouragement of a more mature nearby community. We have also maintained close contact with concerned parents and pastors who willingly lend assistance, advice, and correction. Our community, however, is governed entirely by itself; its leadership is derived from within. Most of the community live at home with their families, but some who have finished high school are beginning to form households. Interestingly enough, an increasing number of those graduating from high school are choosing to remain in the city for further schooling or work rather than leaving the area. A great percentage of those going away to college, however, are careful to select schools where there is an existing community. Among those who have remained, several have reduced school and work loads, when necessary, to be of more service to the community and their church.

Perhaps one of the greatest obstacles God had to deal with in my ministry is the desire I have for perfection which tends to make me unwilling to trust others, especially younger people, with responsibility. Dying to myself in this area meant letting someone else perform a task or function when I believed I could do it better; allowing another with less experience to counsel someone when I felt the solution bursting inside me; asking a younger brother to give a teaching, knowing full well that it would not be as clear as I liked. It also meant standing with them when they failed, pointing out what was good and what needed to be changed and how to go about changing it. It meant correcting others at times, but sometimes saying nothing in order to let them learn on their own. It meant allowing and encouraging others to correct me, admitting when I was wrong, and asking forgiveness when needed.

Dying to self also meant sometimes admitting to others that I did not know what to do with their problem or situation, but assuring them that God did and that he would help us figure it out together, thereby pledging myself to stand with them until things were resolved. It meant maintaining a commitment to others even in the midst of discouraging situations compounded by "more promising opportunities" elsewhere. Hardest of all, it meant letting some who looked up to me in on the secrets and struggles of my life. As one might suspect, the greater the death to self, the greater the life in return.

One last important aspect of my ministry with youth pertains to our being able to have fun together. We love the Lord deeply and enjoy times of prayer and sharing; we take seriously Christ's mission and that of his Church; but we also find a personal sense of fulfillment as individuals and as a body in having fun. Although we vary widely in age and background, God has enabled us all to enjoy being together in relaxed, seemingly unspiritual atmospheres such as parties, dinners, picnics, and activities of all sorts. It has often been only in these situations that there was the right opportunity for brothers and sisters to penetrate thick walls of fear, suspicion, and tension. Unfortunately, the evil one has so distorted the purposes and methods of having fun in our society that, like affection, fun is often considered inconsistent with spiritual maturity. As we have allowed God to graciously provide us with the healthy means of having fun and receiving affection, we have in turn found ourselves as young single people far less tempted to reach for the poisonous fruit that the world offers.

As I look back, the major tool God has used in forming my ministry is the truth of his Word as it has been applied to my life. Utilizing someone else's principles or methods has only worked as they were refined by personal application, evaluation, and restatement. The most effective areas of ministry for me are those that I have had to struggle with personally. As God dealt with weaknesses in my life and made me strong, I was then able to be used uniquely by him to help others with those same weaknesses. They in turn are specially "ordained" to help others, and God's system of love and care expands to include those of every age in his Church where we are all called to encourage one another until he returns.

Healing of a Country: a Beginning

By R. Douglas Wead

If peace ever comes to Northern Ireland, I believe it will be through the power of the Holy Spirit which is beginning to sweep that land. While the scene of Catholics and Protestants singing "we are one in the Spirit" may be commonplace in other parts of the world, it is no less than a miracle in Northern Ireland.

A renewal movement has begun to take hold. Irish Catholic and Protestant prayer groups are meeting, although cautiously. It is a start.

No one can fully appreciate what the Holy Spirit is now doing in Ulster without an understanding of how desperate the situation has been. Eight hundred years of denominational rivalry, of political, economic, and social conflict have polarized Irish Protestants and Catholics. Over the past four years alone the hosility has yielded at least 390 deaths and a minimum of 7,300 wounded.

Though much of the violence has been perpetrated by a minority of Catholics and Protestants, that minority has paralyzed the tiny province. While researching and preparing a manuscript on Northern Ireland, I sought out various opinions from militant leaders, clergymen, and members of Parliament.

The Catholics

Catholics are understandably bitter about voter and job discrimination. Though political changes have been taking place at tremendous speed by Irish standards, most of the Catholics we talked to were suspicious.

In the ghettos, families still seemed to live under the thumb of the militant Irish Republican Army (I.R.A.). One family we visited had 20 German Mauser machine guns which they were to keep until further notice.

British-Catholic hostility was real. In one incident my driver was pulled from the vehicle by soldiers. They slugged him in the mouth and might have done more if my American accent and press pass had not caught them by surprise.

One of the homes we visited in the Catholic area, called Lower Falls Road, was that of Mr. and Mrs. John Nugent. The Nugents have 11 children, including a fifteen-year-old son Kieren. Two days before we visited, Kieren Nugent and his friend Barney McLaren were machine-gunned by Protestant militants. Barney died instantly. Kieren Nugent, whose body took eight bullets, had miraculously lived. The alleged assassins, whom Kieren identified, were free on bond. After spending considerable time trying to determine the motive behind this shooting, we finally concluded that it was simply because he was a Catholic.

The Protestants

Protestants fear a united Ireland. They fear the

Catholics would dominate such a government. While Protestants allow Catholic worship in Ulster, they fear a united Ireland would not respect Protestant religious views. Birth control might become illegal, and they would probably have to pay taxes to support a school system that would teach their children Catholic doctrines. They also fear papal supremacy. Some Protestants believe that a Catholic government can be influenced by a Pope who might act in the interest of international Catholicism at their expense.

Although some Irish Catholic and Protestant fears may appear naive, they are very real. I began to realize that when Tommy Herron was murdered.

Tommy Herron was the vice chairman of the Ulster Defense Association and a colorful spokesman for the Protestant militant views. He gave one of my researchers a tour of Belfast.

"Do you see that housing development over there?" he asked. "That cost millions of dollars. Now it's a pigsty. The Catholics moved in. They're lazy. They won't work. They go on welfare. They use their doors to burn in their fireplaces."

Two months after our last interview with Herron, he disappeared. Three days later his dead body was found in a ditch. A victim of the I.R.A.? No. Tommy Herron was murdered by members of a rival Protestant organization. Why? It was because he was considered a "moderate." By militant Protestant standards, he was accused of being "too soft" on Catholics.

The British

It took the English almost 500 years to control

Ireland, and it may be that long before she becomes independent again.

The British Army receives abuse from the Catholics and the Protestants. Ian Paisley, a member of British Parliament and a strong anti-Catholic, complained that the Army is prejudiced against Protestants. Yet, stories abound of soldiers destroying property in the Catholic ghettos.

By special permission from British headquarters at Lisburn, I joined an army foot patrol in the New Lodge Road area. Bottles and rocks were hurled at us. An old man spit at us from his window.

Most of the young British soldiers were numbed by the hatred around them. We investigated an incident which involved four British sergeants who had been lured to their deaths by two young girls working for the Catholic I.R.A. Though some refer to this as a religious war, three of the four assassinated soldiers were Catholic and the fourth was a Protestant married to a Catholic.

A British senior press officer told me, "If they want us to go home, all they have to do is learn to get along together and we will leave."

Although Ireland's traditional Pentecostals can trace their beginnings to the early 1900's, it wasn't until January 10, 1971, that a Catholic charismatic prayer group began in Dublin. Before this time classical Pentecostals had been polarized into the Protestant camp, but in 1971 the Holy Spirit, in his quiet and gentle way, began uniting Irish Catholics and Protestants.

A small group of Catholics and Protestants began meeting regularly in Dublin to pray for peace and renewal in Ireland. Soon the movement spread to Belfast. The Rev. Cecil Kerr, chaplain of Queens University there, first became acquainted with the renewal through Rev. Graham Pulkingham from Redeemer Episcopal Church in Houston, Texas. In 1971, Pulkingham and members of his staff visited Belfast. Initially, Kerr was cautious. However, months later, while visiting the United States, he attended prayer services at Redeemer Church in Houston.

Amazed at what he saw, Kerr returned to Belfast anxious to see such a renewal on his campus. Not only did a prayer group begin at Queens University, but over the next two years dozens of prayer groups were formed in cities throughout Ireland.

And the renewal continues to grow. In January, 1973, a small group of Irish Catholics and Protestants met at Benburb, North Ireland, for the country's first charismatic conference. Leader Larry Kelly called it a "historic" weekend because Catholics and Protestants were singing the same songs and praising God together. A second conference was held in the spring of 1973 with more than 300 delegates attending.

Renewal continues. Jesus Christ is at the center of attention. Perhaps the Holy Spirit will demonstrate in Northern Ireland that love truly is stronger than hate.

Asia: Report from New Guinea

By Maria F. von Trapp

Q. Maria, how did you become interested in becoming a missionary in New Guinea?

M. Since I was a little girl I've always had a desire to be a missionary. One time when we were on a singing tour to Australia I met a missionary on sick leave from New Guinea and the desire grew. When we stopped singing as a group in 1956, as different members of the family had more children and took different directions, I felt like it was the time to go.

Q. What has your role been in New Guinea?

M. Well, I work with a group of people, priests and nuns, on Fergusson Island, which is in the Papua section of New Guinea which belongs to Australia. I help in singing, teaching, medical work, cooking, basically in whatever's needed. I feel like this is where God wants me and the natives and we are like a family. There are about 13,000 people on the island and most are either Catholic or Methodist.

Q. What's going on spiritually in the missions in New Guinea today?

M.   Well, we're trying very hard, but I would say that something has gone flat in the past five years. We work hard at preparing people for baptism, but after they're baptized they return to their old ways of life. It's seemed like we ourselves didn't have the strength of Christian life to communicate effectively to others.

We in the missions today are looking for something to help us in effectively communicating Christianity, I would say now that we are looking for the Holy Spirit and how to help others receive him. I would say that the missionaries and missions need the Holy Spirit very badly. The Holy Spirit is the only answer.

Q.   We've heard that several members of what were the Trapp Family Singers have become deeply involved in the charismatic renewal and that you are among them. Could you tell us a little about how you have become involved?

M.   Since I've been home on leave my sister Agathe (an interview with Agathe was published in the October issue) would call me up every week from Baltimore where she had been involved to tell me about it. As I got to see the changes the Holy Spirit was making in Agathe's life, I knew this was for real and for me. Agathe is truly a different person, much more free and open and joyful than ever.

Q.   What has being baptized in the Spirit meant in your life?

M.   For me it was a rather quiet experience with no

strong emotional effects. Over a period of time I
gradually began to feel much closer to the Lord.
Speaking in tongues really helped in this, although at
first I thought that I just had a few silly syllables and
was not confident it really was from the Lord. But
one night when I was babysitting for Johannes'
baby, a stream of Chinese sounding syllables began
to come and convince me that it was from the Lord.
Now I feel a lot stronger pull towards the Lord himself, and Scripture which before was boring now
speaks to me. In the process I have stopped smoking
and when I feel low or down I read some book from
the charismatic renewal or the New Testament and
it helps quite a bit.

Q.   Would you like to say anything to your brothers
and sisters in the renewal here before you return to
New Guinea?

M.   I would like them to pray for me and for the
missions, that I may become free in sharing the
great gifts of God, and that the missions may know
that it is the Holy Spirit whom they seek. Missionaries are killing themselves today for what is
often the wrong reason. Some are full of energy and
knowledge and work hard but don't know what they
have to give. One priest I know wants to become a
doctor to be able to give something to the natives.
He does not know that he has Christ to give. Others
are very shy and don't know how to share Christ
with others. Both need the Holy Spirit. I can't tell
you how much the missions need the Holy Spirit.

The Poor, the Rich and the Kingdom

By Fr. Rick Thomas

One of the major sins of our times is greed. Our whole lives are shot through with greed and built on the desire to acquire and possess more than we need. Our church is guilty of this sin; our society is guilty of this sin; our political system is guilty of this sin. We humans rape nature—the water, the air, the land, everything—seeking a profit, as if the water, the wildlife, the countryside, the beauty, were ours to exploit. The U.S. spends billions of dollars on defense to protect our way of life, our freedom. We talk about other, noble freedoms; but the freedom that many of us desire on the gut level is the freedom to possess and be greedy. I have often wanted to preach God's word about greed, but I usually lack the courage: it would be too contrary to what people want to hear. Jesus' word in Luke's Gospel is *"none of you can be my disciples unless he gives up all his possessions."*

Rely on Yahweh

The idea that material possessions can give any kind of security has no support whatsoever from Scripture. In fact, Scripture teaches that we need to break with our possessions to find our true security in God. As God led his chosen people out of Egypt and through the desert, he fed them with manna. God told them to go out in the morning and gather enough for the day but no more. Some gathered more, hoping to have security for the next day: but whatever extra they gathered spoiled. God was telling them, and he tells us, that he will provide everything day-by-day if we trust him. The chosen people were to have God as their portion, God as their inheritance. For many of us, God is not our primary trust: we trust money. If we have money, we have security and do not have to trust God for our daily sustenance as the Israelites did. We look for our security in the things that God has loaned us for the building of his kingdom.

A way to trust God is built into the Old Testament laws. In the seventh year there was to be no planting and no harvesting of crops. Food was to be put in the common storehouse each year: God promised that in the seventh year there would be plenty of food to carry them through into the eighth year. There were also laws to keep anyone from being destitute. An owner was not allowed to harvest his crop completely: he'd have to leave the sides of his fields to be harvested by the alien and the poor. Further, a person could not acquire a great deal of land, because every seventh year the original owner or members of his family could claim the property back. The whole system was set up to keep anybody from getting too acquisitive or too rich. Following God's detailed law, the nation and the individual would come to to trust God for their material needs.

The two great sins that the Hebrew People committed were unfaithfulness to God through idolatry, and failure to seek social justice. It was often greed that led them into idolatry. Casting their children into Moloch's fire or going through a fertility rite were thought to bring more wealth and security. Today we bypass Moloch: money can buy all the things we or our children need. We skip the worship of this or that idol, and go directly to money. But God's message is still, "*I* am the only God; you don't need any security besides me." As followers of God we should put our trust in him, and not in what he made (Matthew 6:33).

The New Testament

Our seeking after material possessions is a great obstacle to doing God's work. When Jesus sent his Twelve to proclaim the reign of God, it was without staff, bag, bread, or money (Luke 9:3). Deprived of all, they would have to trust God every step of the way. It takes faith to put this kind of trust in God. If I have a wallet full of money, cashier's checks, and a bank account, it is a lot easier to feel secure. That's the way we have been taught to think, but it is different from the evangelical trust Jesus wanted his disciples to have.

Jesus proclaimed this trust in the Sermon on the Mount. Look at the birds of the air. They do not sow, or reap, or gather into barns—your Father feeds them. Look at the lilies of the field. They do not make clothes or worry—God clothes them, beautifully. How much more you of little faith. The faith he spoke of was faith in God's providence. He will take care of our needs if we seek his kingdom first. Yet we are tempted to take care of our material needs first; then we will have time to work for the

Church. Or we feel that when we have plenty of material security, then we will give money to the poor.

Many people are in severe pain for years because they cannot afford to buy a prescription. Many don't eat properly. The clear teaching of Scripture is that we are aliens on God's property and stewards of his riches. In the Acts of the Apostles, the early Christians sold what they had and gave it to the apostles so that everyone's needs could be met. The Fathers of the Church said the goods that are left over after our needs are met *belong* to the poor. This sounds shocking, but we are only God's stewards.

The Neighbor

The two great commandments are to love God with our whole mind, our whole heart, and our whole soul, and to love our neighbor as ourselves. In answer to the lawyer's question about who is a neighbor, Jesus spoke the parable of the good Samaritan (Luke 10:30). This parable is an illustration of the second of the two great commandments: *how* we love our neighbor and *who* our neighbor is. The two main characters in the parable were political enemies, living in different countries. They were also religious enemies: to both hatred of the other was a part of their religious practice. The Samaritan gives his enemy personal medical attention and puts him up at a hotel. It's very costly in time, convenience, and money; he sets his own plans aside. It is also a long-term help; he tells the innkeeper to continue to look after him and that he will come back and pay more money if necessary.

We can quibble and ask how wide a road must

be before one is excused from crossing over to a person in need. We can say, "Well, that problem is in another country, or another religion, or another race; it isn't my business." But there is scarcely a road so wide or a distance so great that it excuses us from coming to the aid of our neighbor in need. We cannot look at the great needs of the underdeveloped nations and say, "Why don't *they* do something?"

Consider the priest who first saw the injured man by the side of the road. Probably he said to himself, "I am a priest: I have religious duties: I do not have time." The excuse seemed a good one, even a religious one. The second man was a Levite, a professional priest-helper. He too could have had a religious excuse for not helping the wounded man—he had to help the priest in the temple. But Jesus rejected the conduct of these two.

Many people, even Church people, accept what our society teaches: "Help yourself to everything you can, and everything you can possibly want. Then give a token to your neighbor in need; it is nice to help the missions and the orphans." Tokenism has nothing to do with loving our neighbor as ourself. If we really loved our neighbor as ourself, we would be interested in seeing that he ate as well as we eat ourselves, and that he had as good a house and education as our own.

How?

Social problems are so complex and so vast and so interlocked that they stagger the mind. There is no simple solution to the world's problems of poverty, starvation, injustice. Often when we solve one problem, we cause many more. For example, a law raising the minimum wage will benefit some people but many others may lose their jobs when employers can't afford the added expense. The intent of the law is to raise wages and help people live a better life; but it might have just the opposite effect for many people, putting them in a desperate situation.

Since the social problem is so complex and interlocked, what can we do? We must first admit our sin, and admit our need for a savior. Jesus is the only one who can straighten the mess out. We must call upon him and ask him to do it, both as individuals and as members of the Church and of this society and of this nation. We must repent personally and corporately and call each other to repentance. Repentance is more than striking our breasts: it is changing our direction. Repentance doesn't mean striking our breasts as we reach for more material possessions and more comfort. We must also make ourselves and whatever he has given us available to Jesus. This means our whole lives, all our possessions—for him to use in any way he wants in a solution to the world-wide problem.

We live in a society that shields us from knowing what tragic things go on. Some of us never smell poverty; we never bury a person who dies of malnutrition. But misery and tragedy exist very close to where even the richest of us live. Within a mile of where I go to sleep, people freeze to death every year. I live in a city where making clothes is a major industry.

Christians should live frugally in order to put their possessions at God's service. This is especially true of religious with a vow of poverty; but all Christians are called to put their comforts on the line, and share them with those who do not have the basic necessities of life. If everybody in the world was living decently, there would be room for luxury.

There is one further complexity to our social problems that needs to be faced. Sin and greed are not the whole story.

The Enemy

In the whole social question, it is important to remember that "Our battle is not against human forces but against the principalities and powers, the rulers of this world of darkness, the evil spirits in regions above" (Ephesians 6:12). Jesus often spoke of the power of Satan in the world. Though that power was broken with the crucifixion and resurrection, the Prince of this world can still dominate social systems. He knows that if he can keep whole systems in his slavery, many people will live in vice and despair, sadness and sorrow, and will never find Jesus. The devil and his helpers cause people to sin, to be sick, to suffer, and to live in poverty, by fostering unjust and evil systems that perpetuate all these things. As individuals are afflicted, tempted and abused by spirits of various kinds, so are systems and nations under bondage. Many Christians are part of business enterprises under the control of and supported by the Prince of this world.

In social problems, this is the nature of the struggle. People who have worked for social justice realize how frustrating it can be. Sometimes they can work for years and produce nothing. Or they reach some goal, and see that they have really accomplished nothing. They have replaced one set of oppressors with another, or they may have tinkered with the social system but not made any substantial change. They may have been frustrated for years trying to do a very simple thing. Feeding the poor seems like a very simple thing, but can be blocked for years in a way that cannot be explained naturally. If someone were going to build a tavern or a house of prostitution, it could be done with little money and no obstacles. Try to do something useful, and there are countless obstacles one after the other.

Weapons

Since a main objective in the social apostolate is to correct bad institutions, and since the nature of the battle is spiritual, we have to use spiritual weapons. One of these weapons is to praise God, that his power be released to break the power of Satan in men's lives and in the systems that keep people in bondage. Another weapon is the expectancy of God's salvation. We must live, praying and believing, that Jesus will save us from the mess that we have made of the world.

Another spiritual weapon is the exorcism of the Church. The Roman Ritual includes an exorcism of a community "to be delivered from every influence of the accursed spirits, from their every evil snare and deception." Pope Leo XIII wanted all Catholics in the world to say this exorcism daily. It is interesting to note that the same Leo XIII was the first modern pope to speak about social problems in unequivocal language.

Other weapons we need are the charismatic gifts. I think new charismatic gifts are coming to help us in this battle. I expect people to emerge with gifts we never thought about, gifts to come to grips with social problems and come against the spiritual powers that keep the world in bondage. We certainly need people with the gift of wisdom and understanding to see through the practical difficulties. When I read in the Mexican paper that several people were frozen to death in the freightyards, I say to myself, "Well, I have to go help these people. I have a coat that I could give to somebody." Then the practical problem comes up: how am I going to find the man that needs this coat? There are hundreds who would sell the coat to buy a bottle of wine. The gifts of knowledge and understanding are charismatic gifts that God has to give his people if they are going to cooperate in the building of his kingdom on earth. I look for these gifts, not familiar now, to emerge.

I believe that the charismatic renewal is preparing the body of Christ for the ministry of healing society. The charismatic renewal can motivate people to give themselves to working for the poor and the correction of social evils. Motivation is a prime factor. You cannot pay people and get them to make significant headway, at least in my experience. It is a fallacy to think that money equals progress. The motivation comes from Jesus, not from money. The charismatic renewal is already motivating many people to give themselves to this type of service.

The charismatic renewal is also able, I believe, to call people to effective evangelical poverty. Christians must be willing to share their lives and their possessions with the poor and needy. The renewal already has shown itself capable of creating Christian communities that are able to deal with these problems, or, at least, show promise of being able to deal with these problems effectively. Hopefully, the charismatic renewal will also have power to renew religious congregations and call them back to a life of evangelical poverty, and give up the hypocrisy and the bondage of Satan in which they now find themselves.

The charismatic renewal will enable people to fight the spiritual warfare that exists in the social apostolate. We must fight the powers of Satan in individuals who are afflicted and also in evil systems, institutions, and governments that are bound by the evil one. We have had experience with individuals, but no successful experience yet of conquering Satan's widespread influence in social systems. Hopefully that success won't be too long coming.

Removing Racial and Social Barriers

By Capt. T. David Parham, U.S.N.

In 1945 I was at Manana Barracks, Hawaii with an unusual concentration of black American sailors. There were 3000 of them within a barbed wire fence; the barbed wire turned inward, with armed guards patrolling the fence. The guards were white American sailors. Liberty expired at 6 o'clock every evening including Sundays. The men were transported to the docks to unload the ships in cattle cars. They were returned to the barracks before dark in the same cattle cars, where they were safely penned up for the night lest we should have a recurrence of a riot that had shaken Hawaii, had been repeated on Guam, repeated in Saipan, and, it was feared, would have repercussions back in the United States.

I was one of three chaplains there, and I knew the tension, I knew the suspicion, I knew the distrust the men felt for the commanding officer and all of the other officers who did not have the same paint job as we did. And I knew that one act, one word out of place, one rumor of an incendiary nature would throw the whole thing into confusion, hostility, and combat that would do no one any good. I didn't know what to do.

Fortunately, the men could go to church. So we went to church every night seven nights a week. We began to visit the churches on the island, one right after the other. I remember going into one church where the pastor was a woman, Sister Mahoy. The music was loud. They had instruments that the 150th psalm hadn't even thought about. After the sermon there was an altar call during which Sister Mahoy came around behind and prayed for each person who went forward. When she got behind one of the sailors, Brother Abraham Houston, something happened to Brother Houston, and he began to make sounds which seemed like Chinese to us. And Sister Martha, a Portuguese girl kneeling next to him, also began to make sounds that I'd never heard before.

The next night, we went to another chapel which was in the civilian housing area. There the preacher was a Pentecostal. He was a sailor, a third-class cook, Brother Burns. I had never heard such a sermon. He told us to look for Jesus and he told us where to look: he told us to look up, and he spoke in terms of the heavenly regions to which Jesus had ascended. Then he told us to look around us, and he spoke of the saints who form that cloud of witnesses who are responsive to our needs, and whose hearts yearn with ours as we make this heavenly pilgrimage. After this sermon, Brother Houston jumped out of his seat, a black man from Newark, New Jersey, where they had riots and blood flowing in the streets just a few years ago, and he ran up to this third-class Pentecostal cook, a white man from Tennessee, where 16 years ago I was refused accommodations in a motel, and they locked themselves in the bear hug that is so characteristic of this renewal.

I sat there with my mouth open, and wondered what these things meant.

Now, almost thirty years later, I know what these things mean. I believe that I was seeing just the beginning of what would happen here in this day and time, as under the influence of the Holy Spirit people are forgetting backgrounds, forgetting ethnic identification, forgetting ancient wrongs and hurts, as they echo the words of John Wesley, "If your heart feels as my heart, give me your hand."

There is a possibility of removing racial and social barriers through just the type of renewal which we are seeing today. It's practically impossible to stand and praise the Lord with hands uplifted next to somebody different from you in every respect, turn and embrace him with the holy kiss of the New Testament, and maintain after that any hostility, any grievance, any resentment, or any suspicion against him whose life has been filled even as yours has and is overflowing with love and compassion for our common concerns.

When I was filled with the Spirit I had a vision of Jesus stretched on the cross for my sins. I saw the blood and the water pouring from his side—not in trickles, but like a fire hydrant. It swept away the devil who stood there waiting for me, claiming me. And in that torrent I forgot the hurt of the motel in Tennessee, the hurts of a boyhood in North Carolina, the rejection at a learned university in that state when I wanted to go to seminary and had to go to Pittsburgh instead, and the stories that my grandfather could tell of his life as a slave; that my other grandparents could tell of their lives in Virginia. So now, these things don't matter any more. It's a new life, it's a new world, it's a new experience in the Spirit of God, who indeed has torn down the middle wall of division, and has made us all one in a sense that I never expected to see, much less to participate in. My wonder is that we can love and enjoy each other's presence the way we do; being born in opposite camps, with positions of hostility on both sides.

There is the inherent possibility and also the urgent obligation of charismatic Christians to move into this area of social concern in word and deed. We have the advantage of the structuring of the charismatic community in intimate fellowship groups which can bridge the normal social and economic gaps which we find in our society. The Full Gospel Business Mens Fellowship, for example, embraces those from all the denominations. Richard Nielwin traces American denominational trends to social distinctions. It enfolds Carlyle Marney's "inside outsider" as well as the "outside outsider." My survey last month of 50 prominent religious bodies showed many renewal groups to be in the forefront of the crusade for social reconciliation. I'm sure the racial and social barriers will not only fall, but they'll disappear, and in years to come, we'll wonder if they ever were.

In 1928, at North Carolina Central University I listened to Edwin Markham recite a poem which he had written. "He drew a circle that shut me out— heretic, rebel, a thing to flout. But Love and I had the wit to win: We drew a circle that took him in!" This is what the charismatic fellowship, the charismatic circle, is going to do to the barriers that had tried to separate us.

More for Liberia

By Torre and Jean Bissell

Torre and Jean Bissell left the United States in 1966 to do missionary teaching work for the Episcopal Church in Nigeria. During the Nigerian Civil War in 1967 they were evacuated and reassigned to a mission station in Robertsport, Liberia, in West Africa.

They taught there for four years but grew increasingly discouraged because they saw little change through their work. Returning to the United States they were determined not to go back to mission work until something had happened in their own lives to give them power to serve. In the United States they learned about the charismatic renewal and prayed to be baptized in the Holy Spirit. They returned to Africa in 1971 to Cuttington College in Suacoco, Liberia.

They describe here the difference the baptism in the Spirit has made in their mission work; they also tell some of what the Holy Spirit is doing to renew all of Liberia.

In all of our time in Liberia Jean and I have sensed that its people are in great need of the power of the Gospel. Only 15% of all Liberians are Christian; 10% are Muslims and 74% are Animists. In

Animism, every tree or hill or stream is seen as having its own individual spirit. A really big tree would have a big spirit and would tend to be worshipped, as would a big mountain.

The practice of witchcraft is widespread among the tribal cultures in large parts of West Africa and because of it there is a basic mistrust among individuals—a mistrust that exists at all levels of society. If a man wants to obtain something important to him such as another wife or a high-paying job, he will go to the religious man of the village, a kind of shaman or diviner. The diviner might even tell him that he has to sacrifice a member of his own family in order to get what he wants. This is usually done by poisoning. So even though the extended family system is in one sense very close, people frequently will live in terror of each other.

Although Christian teaching has penetrated into Liberia in numerous missionary and local Christian schools, there has been some difficulty in communicating the full Gospel to the tribal people. It is not uncommon for people to be baptized and confirmed without ever being called to radically reorient their lives around Jesus Christ as their Lord, and to ask for the power of the Spirit. As one author put it, they have been sacramentalized but not evangelized.

In addition, some missionaries have tended to play down the work of evil spirits even to the point of saying they don't exist. This causes a difficulty for tribal people, who know they do exist and have to contend with them as a regular part of their daily life. Since the Christianity they have learned has no way of dealing with evil spirits, they revert to the traditional tribal methods for that part of their life, and in doing so they get into further bondage with the evil one.

After seeing in the charismatic renewal the powerful work of the Holy Spirit in all aspects of people's lives, we were sure that the Lord had more, also, for the people of Liberia. When we returned to Liberia after being baptized in the Spirit, our eyes were opened to how much more the Lord wanted to give and how ready he was to give it.

I remember one particular incident that showed me how freeing a fuller understanding of the Gospel can be for these people. One night, I called up John, a fellow staff member, and asked if his house boy, Flumo, could take a message to a nearby village for me. Flumo was about twelve or thirteen years old. John said that Flumo didn't want to go because the policemen of that village had just seen a Ginii near the house where I wanted the message sent. A Ginii is a sort of ghost spirit figure that could capture and control a person. Everybody in the village was afraid and nobody would go there. I didn't want to press the matter so I hung up. After a few minutes I called John back and asked if Flumo was a Christian. When I found out he was, I said, "Tell Flumo that there is power in the name of Jesus." John told me later that Flumo gulped and said okay, he would go, but asked if he could please borrow John's flashlight. Armed with the power of the name of Jesus and John's flashlight, he went off to deliver the message. He had found a new freedom in being told about the power of Jesus to handle spirits. It's no small thing for an African kid to be able to go off at night where he's convinced a Ginii is lurking.

Another incident happened shortly after we had

returned to Liberia. It started when Fr. Tom, a young priest of the Church of England, stayed overnight in our home. He was at a crisis point in his faith, and felt desperate. We talked with him until about two o'clock in the morning, telling him how the Lord had worked in our own lives and in the lives of the people around us. After he left us he learned that a student he was helping had gone completely out of his mind. At least partially as a result of what we had shared with Tom, he found faith to go and help the student.

Fr. Tom found him in a village chained to a log. He was uncontrollably violent except for a few hours in the morning, and had been drinking his own urine, an ultimate sign of madness in the tribal culture. Before Fr. Tom came, the local Christians had prayed for the boy, but he had just gotten worse. A psychiatrist that Fr. Tom consulted diagnosed the student as schizophrenic and possessed with an evil spirit.

After feeding him some tranquilizers, Tom positioned himself just outside of the student's reach. He started talking to him by holding up a cross and asking, "Do you see this, do you know what it is?" The student would groggily tune in and recognize it, and then they would carry on a conversation. The student gradually described how he had been possessed by an evil spirit one night and had the schizophrenic break.

Later Tom asked the congregation in a nearby town to pray for the student. He remembered the passage in Scripture where Jesus says that some demons come out only *"by prayer and fasting,"* so he had the congregation prepare by praying and fasting for a whole week. When the student was carried in to be prayed with, all the people from the church gathered around him. They all prayed with the laying on of hands for him to be delivered, and the demon was cast out as they prayed. He stood up in the middle of the congregation in his right mind and told them what had happened. A kind of thrill went through the whole area because of this.

In addition to these incidents, we have seen real signs of hope for Liberia in the work of the Spirit through "God Power." The young Methodist bishop of Liberia who died last year had a vision of the church being renewed and becoming more active in evangelistic outreach. As a result, interested clergy and laymen in the Methodist church have started a campaign called "God Power." It is designed to renew the church with the power of God through basic teaching about the work of the Holy Spirit.

As part of the program, students from the Methodist seminary were sent out two by two into various Methodist churches to preach the Gospel. In preparation, they spent a week studying the book of Acts, and praying together. On the final night they had an all-night prayer vigil, asking for the power of the Holy Spirit on their ministry.

When they went out they had remarkable success. One student was sent to preach in his home region, which was hostile to Christianity. Just a few months earlier, the student's father was severely beaten for becoming a Christian. His father was a Zoe—a religious tribal figure who is in charge of all the traditions of the men or the women. His fellow tribesmen were enraged because he threw away his Zoe paraphernalia when he became a Christian.

The student's friends warned him that the next village on their route was very hostile to Christianity. They tried to convince him not to go, but he went anyway. As he preached, many from the village gathered around and there was a lot of heckling. When he was finished speaking, he asked if anyone wanted to become a Christian. After a long pause, a small boy of about 10 or 12 years came forward; at that point the student wasn't sure what to do but he decided to pray with the boy there. After he finished, a number of adults came forward and asked how to become Christians.

That night, four Zoes from the village had an identical dream about being left out when all the people of the village were going someplace good. They each knew they had to go to this student to find out more, and they all met one another on the way as they came to him secretly by night. The boy taught them how to become Christians, and they were baptized.

Another young student was preaching in a different area, and came across an old married couple who were about to break up. Both thought that all these years they had been holding on to one another by magic. They feared that the magic was no longer working since they felt they were growing apart. The student was able to talk to them about Christ and counsel them. He brought them back together and showed them that they loved each other without the magic. In the end, they flushed their magic medicine down the toilet together. The woman kept saying to the student, "I could have borne you two or three times over, and here you are giving us wisdom."

There were several other married couples reconciled on these preaching tours, and three or four paralytics were healed. However, the largest general result of these missions was to bring back, not only to the church but to Christ, people who had fallen away.

In addition, God Power's simple teaching about the Holy Spirit has been a great help in opening up people in the larger denominations to the powerful work of the Holy Spirit. Many have shied away from prophecy and the other spiritual gifts because the gifts have often been badly misused and corrupted. They have been excited to hear that the Lord also gives discernment to tell which is the Holy Spirit and which is the work of another spirit.

We feel that the Lord is bringing about the spiritual renewal to the whole church in Liberia, and we believe that what we have seen so far is just a taste of what the Holy Spirit intends to do there. We think he is setting about to show all of Liberia how much he cares about its people and how much power he is willing to give Christians to bring freedom and new life to all.

A New Vision for Missionaries

By Fr. Charles Magsam

After many years in which the function and the purpose of the whole missionary effort were questioned and strongly attacked, the Lord is revealing a glimpse of an exciting future. After years of isolation and frustration, a new hope, born of the Spirit of God, is coming forth among missionaries. A fresh wind is blowing away the clouds; we are getting a new vision of our life and work. The same vision that Jesus communicated to Nicodemus one dark night, the same word he speaks to every Christian, is taking root and producing fruit in the lives of many of the missionaries I know.

Nicodemus was competent, well informed in things religious and a deeply good man, but he was horrified at the threat of having to surrender his minutely programmed life for a new freedom which demanded that he be at the delicately insistent call of a Spirit he hardly knew and whose leading could be as invisible and unpredictable as the wind. He expressed his surprise and shock by a childish reply.

There is something of Nicodemus in all of us. We are all nourished by accustomed ways that are deeply rooted in our feelings. Usefulness, official sanction, and the comfort of the familiar have so much become our inner self that we would scarcely recognize ourselves without them, and we feel any threat to them as a threat to our very person.

More than we know, we have surrendered freedom, initiative, and vitality to what is largely transitory and relative. More than we know, we are crippled prisoners, even though the key to the prison door rests unnoticed in our very hands. God never meant us to be limited, hampered, and timid. We have sold ourselves cheaply: we need to relearn the way to freedom. God sent his Son to be an overwhelming revelation to his fatherly tenderness toward us and of his confidence in us. He wants to teach us the great mystery that his Holy Spirit is a divine Person who is also our Spirit. Invisibly and visibly, the Spirit continues what Jesus began.

Vatican II has both called for and exemplified a new freedom, initiative, and vitality that has shocked and disturbed many people into becoming as defensive as Nicodemus. But the rapidly changing world in which we live has taken the initiative for us. Christians are daily challenged by their unstable environment to show the spiritual power needed to humanize and spiritualize the scientific and industrial developments that threaten to escape our control. We must simply decide between remaining frightened and confused slaves of the accustomed and daring to be the Spirit-filled sharers and missioners of God's healing power. Either we will move with the really vital and truly progressive currents of our time or we will be left in the backwash of life.

Actually, through us, God wants to liberate all men from their rigid ways, from false fears and timidity, and free them to proclaim with conviction God's presence and healing power. Why are we hesitant? Do we think that God is so limited that he can work only through the perfect? Only to the degree that we become aware of our own confusion and fears will we be able to face our audacious refusal to take seriously the clear commitments of an Almighty God to work powerfully through us just as we are (1 Cor. 1:19-31, Mark 10:13-16 and 16:15-18, John 14:13-14). God does not need perfect instruments.

While we face our appalling reluctance to take God seriously, we have also to face the inadequacy of any isolated human being to lift himself unaided out of his own loneliness. God never meant man to stand alone. The isolated person is weak, easily discouraged, and quickly defeated. God made men to be the instruments of his tenderness, but by working together with their fellow men. The individualism that may have served another generation is no longer adequate. Only by uniting with others at the deep level of prayer and sacred song (Eph. 5:18-20, Col. 3:16-17), and especially of spontaneous thanksgiving and praise to God, can we regain the conquest of our fears and loneliness. Only by praying together can we regain the freedom, initiative, and vitality we need to be witnesses of Christ's presence, power, and love, recognize our own worth and power for good, and build the environment in which human persons can grow to fullness and in which Christian communities will mature. Within such frequent communion with God and with one another, we will experience the interior and exterior healings that restore us to the image and likeness of God which is our true self and our glory.

This is the new mission frontier across which Vatican II and the prayer of John XXIII have thrust us. Waiting to meet us with thirsty hearts and welcoming embraces are those many, many persons who are especially sensitive and open to God. Religious sociologists bracket them at 15 percent of the population. Certainly there are enough of them to occupy fully all available personnel for the foreseeable future. Ultimately, beyond the foreseeable future but within the scan of our missionary vision, is the bright day when this 15 percent will be sufficiently well formed to provide the leaders who will reach out to another 70 percent. This majority is constituted by those who drift and waver until someone liberates, leads, and stabilizes them where their hearts, health, and spiritual destiny mean them to be.

This is the vision which, in one way or another, is inspiring missioners with a new concept of their role and purpose. This is the vision that is touching the people deeply in several countries across the world. This is the vision that is transforming the mission of La Asuncion, Talcahuano, Chile.

Various Bible study centers had already been functioning for several years but the members had become somewhat tired of merely studying Scripture by means of prepared leaflets. They had profited and grown by their bi-weekly study meetings: they had heard God's Word and were looking for a way to respond. As soon as we explained that the Bible is the living voice of the eternal God speaking to us, and that it is discourteous not to answer when he speaks, they wanted to know what they should do. We told them that they were made to speak to God, not only through printed prayers, but also spontaneously from their hearts and in their own words. They were not used to such a way of praying, except in strictest privacy and in silence; there were the barriers of custom and fear to be overcome, but they wanted to try.

They needed to understand that prayer includes more than petition: thanking and praising God, sharing God's word, singing their confidence and joy through lively hymns, sharing good news as witness to God's presence and action, some brief instruction. In its proper place and way, there would be petitions.

They found quickly that each one who thanked and praised God deepened the faith and joy of everyone else. They wanted and needed to meet weekly in order to be inwardly healed of the wounds of daily living and restrengthened in the experience of community. The meetings provided an environment that helps them to resist the materialism, loneliness, and defensive ingrownness of the environment of work and urban life. Their enthusiasm prompted the pastor to ask that a Cursillo Ultreya be turned into a Bible-prayer meeting. The response to this experience was so positive that it was decided to have a weekly Bible-prayer meeting at the parish level. These parish-level meetings proved such a spiritual help that they continued meeting weekly even during the summer, when most parish activities usually collapse.

A group of young people, mostly children of parents in Bible centers, also wanted their own Bible-prayer group. Within a few months the group took up the apostolate of conducting the Sunday catechism-prayer service for children in two different sections of the parish and have initiated the children into spontaneous prayer. Three Bible-prayer groups have matured to the point that the members not only lead the weekly meeting but even rotate the leadership. Several other groups are in various stages of growth, two of them nearly ready to assume their own leadership.

The immediate fruits of the prayer meetings in personal and community life, urge us, out of human and Christian compassion, to take God's Word seriously. Many have said that never before had they so strongly experienced the presence of God as in these prayer meetings. Consistently, members speak of how each meeting seems to heal and strengthen them and leave them rested and at peace. We have seen personality changes from fear and sadness to confidence and joy; there have been physical healings that medical treatment did not achieve. We have noticed deeper changes both in particular persons and in community spirit in the groups.

The meetings are in no sense in-grown or escapist. Every social need gets prayed for from time to time. The social outreach shows itself in the health of whole families when the mother or father achieves new life through God's healing. The need of people to pray together is vital and social, and expands the social awareness as well as the desire to serve others. Drawing closer to God, they draw closer to one another; deep human bonds are formed that grow into authentic loving communities—our one real hope for a renewed society.

An unexpected and unintended effect of praying together with our people six nights a week, each night with a different group, plus several groups during the afternoon, has been a new sense of closeness to our people—a beautiful blend of mutual understanding, respect, and affection which I have never experienced in any previous apostolate. We pray together and share God's Word in the quietest, simplest possible way as brothers and sisters in Christ and we are warmly aware of this deep spiritual bond. Moreover, this experience has given a new and richer understanding of the meaning and possibilities of the missionary priesthood as well as a new attraction to pray together with others. Further unplanned effects have been a new friendliness and openness among the students in our high school and the opportunity of working with young people in Palestra.

The parish structure, far from inhibiting this expansion in depth, has been precisely the institution which has freed and supported me to reach the people in their homes, where their hearts are. There seems little point to identifying either with their work situation or with their neighborhood because they do not themselves identify with either: they live for and identify with their families and their homes. Moreover, since small Christian communities cannot, by themselves, provide certain important services such as education or economic and neighborhood betterment, they need a service center where they can meet to promote their common good. The parish center can serve these purposes as well as a place of common worship and a locale for the unifying bonds of common entertainment and enjoyment. In all these ways the new grows within the shell of the old, as history and all the laws of organic growth require.

A new Christian community *reality* is emerging in South America. A new vision is stirring men's hearts.

A Barrio in Bogotá

By Gary Seromik

A viable example of genuine Christian community and one of the most hopeful social projects in South America is thriving in Bogotá, Colombia. Located in one of the many *barrios* (poor suburbs) that encircle the city, the community is called *El Minuto de Dios* (The Minute of God) and is the progeny of a dedicated priest, Fr. Rafael García-Herreros.

Fr. García's work with El Minuto de Dios dates back to 1956. Deeply moved by the wretched condition of thousands of poor people in Bogotá who were forced to live without adequate food and clothing in shacks constructed out of scrap tin and cardboard, he decided that the Lord was calling him to work with the poor.

Fr. García began very modestly. Every day he appeared on television for one minute with a family that was in immediate need, described their plight, and begged for help. The program was called "El Minuto de Dios." Gradually people responded. However, as time went on Fr. García realized that something more could be done. He envisioned a new community based on Christian principles, where poor families would live in dignity. "God does not intend for his children to live in bad conditions," Fr.

García notes. His vision gave birth to El Minuto de Dios.

Fr. García began his work in the barrio alone. The Eudist congregation to which he belongs gave him permission to begin his work, but was not willing to give him any help. The first thing that Fr. García did was to build a small three-room house with his own hands. He then moved in a family from the hovel where they were living and helped them to adjust to their new environment. He taught them how to cook, how to sew, and how to keep both themselves and their home clean. Other poor families expressed interest in what Fr. García was doing, and more homes began to spring up in the barrio. Financial support continued to come from appeals that Fr. García made on television, while the prospective residents of El Minuto de Dios contributed whatever skills they had to construct each other's homes.

Fr. Garcia's project didn't meet with everyone's approval. Two attempts were made on his life. One time somebody shot at him. Another time someone tried to kill him by crashing a large truck into his car. Fr. García was attacked by both the Communists and the rightists. The Communists considered him their worst enemy because he, a Catholic priest, was doing things for the poor that they had repeatedly promised but never accomplished. The rightists branded Fr. García's community development project as communistic.

This period of his life was characterized by terrible loneliness, Fr. García says. He had absolutely no one to consult with and bore sole responsibility for the consequences of his decisions. Little by little, Fr. García began to see that his efforts were fruitful. Today many of the children of the poor he first helped are now in college and have had their lives completely changed. People who didn't share Fr. García's vision in the beginning and even actively opposed his efforts have come back and begged his forgiveness.

"A Better Life"

Over 10,000 people now live in 2,000 houses that have been built in El Minuto de Dios. Once alone, Fr. García has been joined by top-notch experts in sociology and psychology, architects, engineers, lawyers, and accountants. However, El Minuto de Dios is not merely a conglomeration of houses, but rather the implantation of a style of life based on mutual help. In order to live in the barrio, a family must first of all be in desperate need. Secondly, they must be willing to cooperate with their neighbors. For example, if a man is trained as a carpenter, he is expected to contribute his skill to help his neighbor. Thirdly, a family must be willing to improve their lives physically, intellectually, and morally. Certain rules have been made to help them effectuate this change. Each family must keep their house in repair. If a person is an alcoholic, he must agree to join an Alcoholics Anonymous group that meets in the barrio. Men, women, and children are expected to work one Saturday a month on community projects. Fr. García estimates that 70% of the people in El Minuto de Dios keep the rules very well; the remainder need encouragement from time to time. If for some reason a person is not able to adapt to the life of the community, Fr. García helps them find a good job and a decent living situation outside of the community.

A family that moves into El Minuto de Dios

pays a nominal rent of $3 to $20 a month, depending on the size of their home. If the family pays the rent for five years, the house is theirs. Families who meet their rent without fail and who have proven their willingness to improve their lives may move into a more spacious and comfortable dwelling. Although all housing in El Minuto de Dios is clean and adequate with plumbing and electricity, different houses offer different conveniences. Some are brightly painted frame houses surrounded by small flower gardens. Others are fashioned after small Alsacian houses in France or Andalusian cottages in Spain. Still others offer all the conveniences of modern apartment projects found in the world's major cities.

Fr. Garci'a has taken special care to insure that El Minuto de Dios isn't dependent on him. Every Saturday a meeting is held to discuss community problems, and a democratic government has been set up in the barrio. Every block in the barrio elects a block coordinator. The block coordinators of each of the barrio's ten sections choose a governor for their section. The governors in turn elect a president who serves for six months. Fr. García feels that this system accomplishes effective leadership training among the families of El Minuto de Dios.

Culture in Reach of Everyone

Study, work, recreation, and cultural activities are all integrated aspects of life in El Minuto de Dios. There is a complete school system ranging from kindergarten to secondary school, which all the children in the barrio must attend. Such educational services are not available to all Colombians. Moreover, adults may attend a number of continuing education classes.

In order to bring art to the people, a Museum of Contemporary Art was built in the barrio in 1966. The Museum is considered the vanguard of Colombia's cultural institutions and features many works that have been donated by world-renowned artists. Critics have acclaimed the annual art shows presented at the museum which have helped make the museum a living organism and not simply a sophisticated cemetery of paintings: almost by osmosis people in the barrio have acquired some artistic criteria. In addition, the museum sponsors painting and sculpture workshops for the residents of the barrio.

A theatre with a seating capacity for 700 complements the cultural life of the barrio. Plays, movies, and lectures are regularly presented. Theatre, ballet, and music groups have been formed. El Minuto de Dios will soon begin construction on a media center where books, records, slides, films, and art works will be available on loan to the people.

Athletics also occupy a place of honor: football fields, tennis courts, skating rinks, and a gymnasium have been built.

Workers, not Beggars

A high value is placed on work in El Minuto de Dios. In the early days, signs in the street of the barrio told visitors "Please don't offend families by giving them alms they don't need." "We all know that poorly distributed alms favor poverty and produce beggars," says Fr. Diego Jaramillo, assistant director of El Minuto de Dios. "The hands of man must have a more effective occupation than holding a hat or a tin cup where coins clink as they fall."

Residents of El Minuto de Dios are known for their diligence, and neighboring factories are anxious to employ them. Some small factories have been built in close proximity to the barrio to take advantage of the excellent labor that is available. However, for those who can't find employment outside the barrio, or who have no skills to offer, there is ample opportunity for work within the barrio. Residents staff and administer the schools and offices of the barrio. A cabinet shop, leather shop, textile mill, wood-carving shops, art studios, and construction work offer other employment opportunities for people in the barrio. "Columbia is discovering that its people are gifted with unlimited artistic abilities," Fr. Jaramillo notes. El Minuto de Dios has established a National Center for Artisans to support the artistic endeavors of Colombians. It offers courses that will develop their capabilities and stimulates the sale of their works in three shops that have been opened in Bogotá.

A People of Faith

"Work is important, but more important is the spiritual growth of the people," Fr. Jaramillo says. Members of El Minuto de Dios are completely free to decide whether they want to participate in the barrio's religious activities. However, on their own initiative the people have organized a bi-weekly meeting that is concerned with furthering the spiritual life of the community.

For four years Fr. García offered mass out in the streets because there was no church where he and residents of the barrio could worship. One day, however, a wealthy Colombian gave Fr. García a diamond ring to sell. Proceeds were used to build a church for the barrio, St. John Eudes. The beautiful circular church dominates the barrio, and members now have an appropriate place for worship.

A lot of importance is placed on Chtistian witness, and all community work is centered around the Eucharist and the Word of God. "The desire to announce the Good News, the idea of being a witness of the presence of the Holy Spirit right now in the 20th century, and eagerness to change everything in light of Jesus Christ keeps enthusiasm aflame in El Minuto de Dios," says Fr. Jaramillo.

Every day at 6 a.m. when the day begins, priests from St. John Eudes explain passages from Scripture over the radio. In the evening the Word of God is again commented upon, and Christian attitudes towards daily events are discussed. The programs have always been an effective tool in bringing about social change in the country. Many people remember campaigns that the programs waged in the past against the death penalty, expensive tuition in secondary schools, and the ineffectiveness of Colombian justice. On two occasions, the government ordered Fr. García to stop broadcasting on radio and television, but the order was rescinded when Fr. García went to the president of the country to prove that his statements were true.

Christian witness is also given by the young people of El Minuto de Dios who, during summer vacation, leave with their knapsacks on their backs and preach Jesus in the countryside and villages, or go from door to door in Bogotá inviting people to read the Bible.

A turning point in the spiritual life of El Minuto de Dios occurred a couple of years ago when Fr. García and several other members of the community were baptized in the Holy Spirit. Now every block in the barrio has a prayer group and a Bible study in addition to other activities such as cursillos, Legion of Mary, and the Christian Family Movement. Last Easter an extraordinary event occurred when El Minuto de Dios hosted an evangelistic council for youth. 3000 young people from all over Colombia attended the council, and many experienced Jesus Christ through the Holy Spirit in a powerful way. Afterwards they returned home to proclaim what they had seen and heard, and formed prayer groups and Bible studies. As a result, a silent revolution is occurring among the youth of Colombia which many people believe will transform the religious panorama of the country.

The community is also experimenting with new modes of religious formation which they hope will solve the vocation crisis that Colombia, as many countries of the world, is experiencing today. Two special houses have been set aside for high school and university students within the community who feel that they are being called to the priesthood. These houses operate as minor and major seminaries where study, work, and apostolic action are incorporated in an atmosphere of brotherhood. A congregation of Spanish nuns who work in the barrio maintain a similar house for girls aspiring to religious life. Recently a new course of theological studies was inaugurated for men who would like to be ordained as priests or deacons. The men are able to work in the barrio during the day and study in the evening.

Although most of the people in El Minuto de Dios are Catholic, Fr. García is anxious to foster a sense of ecumenism in the barrio. A few years ago he was joined by Rev. Sam Ballesteros, a Baptist minister from Chula Vista, California. The two men now work side by side. Fr. García envisions the day when Protestant pastors, Catholic priests, Orthodox priests, and Hebrew rabbis will be able to reflect on how the road to God our Father is founded in committing oneself to service of fellow man. Plans are already being made for a "House of Unity" where members of different churches can study and dialogue.

Outreach Programs

The members of El Minuto de Dios have no desire to form a ghetto cut off from the reality of the rest of the country, or separated from it by walls of egoism or unfamiliarity. Consequently, organizations have been established to convey knowledge and skills present in the community to the rest of Colombia. INDEC is a special office which was established to promote community development in rural areas of the country and to help the underdeveloped countryside realize its potential. Other cities in Colombia are also trying to solve their housing problems by using El Minuto de Dios as a model. Another office, Promevi, promotes better housing in Bogotá. When a person asks Promevi for help, the office tries to interest three or four families in the same area in the project. The families then form a small prayer group, and Promevi trains them in various skills that will enable them to augment their financial income. Then the families receive loans from a special bank established by El Minuto de Dios and they help each other build their homes. In the initial stages of construction, high school and university students from

El Minuto de Dios volunteer their weekends to help the families build their homes.

A Third Way

Members of El Minuto de Dios are seeking a lifestyle that overcomes the injustice built into both Capitalism and Communism. "El Minuto de Dios is not seeking richness, but just that people have enough," says Fr. García. Fr. Jaramillo notes that "in El Minuto de Dios everyone enjoys the same opportunities. Regardless of their origin, education, or social background, everyone is a member of the same class: that of working Colombians open to the values of faith, family, and culture."

Fr. García's role as a priest presents no confusion: "This is the best time to be a priest, because the Church is being renewed and the whole world is being renewed."

God's Transforming Power

By Jerry Barker

PART I
How God Worked

In 1954, the year my life changed, I was practic-ing law in Galveston, a city on the Gulf coast about 50 miles from Houston. I had lived all my life in that city; my roots were there. At that time, I was heavily in trial work. This was about four years after I came out of law school and started practicing law with my father and other law partners. I was still fairly young in the law practice. I was trying to find my way and I was under a lot of pressure and tension, particular-ly from home with young children around and that sort of thing. As a result of this, my wife Esther and I went on a week-long retreat conducted by the mis-sionary, Stanley Jones.

During that week there was a point when I real-ly came to know the living presence of the Lord and to experience his life. It was like a whole new dimen-sion had opened up to me. I had been faithfully in-volved in the church—I was even on the vestry of the church at that time—but there had not been a per-sonal relationship with the Lord, a person-to-person knowledge of the Lord Jesus. Now I began to experi-ence this.

I remember that night very well when the Lord became real to me and I began to hear him for the first time. This was such a great revelation to me, to be able to hear his voice speaking to my heart. Later, I began to look at my entire life in this light. I wanted to associate my profession with my commitment to the Lord. I spent a lot of time seeking fellowship with other Christians. I found little fellowship in our own church, so I often went to various places to find Christians who had faith, whom I could talk faith with and share with. There were few people like that in those days. Those were dry days.

The years went by. Those were trying years in many ways because while I really loved the Lord, I did not know very well how to live the Lord's life. There were a lot of trials and testings, ups and downs, but those were still nine years of real faith.

In 1963, I entered a period of terrible difficulty. Since then I've come to see how the Lord often uses difficult times to do a great work in our lives. My wife became very seriously mentally ill and had been placed in a hospital. After careful diagnosis, the doctors told me there was only a limited chance she could return to any sort of normal functioning as a housewife and that I had to face the very distinct likelihood that she would remain a custodial case in some kind of an institution for the rest of her life. As I tried to care for five children, maintain a big house, carry on an active trial practice, as well as carry the burden of my wife's illness, a lot of pressure built up and I began to feel that I had come to the end of my rope. One night, walking back from the hospital after visiting my wife, I started to talk to the Lord. I told him about these problems and I finally said: "You know, Lord, I just don't believe that there's anything that I can do more than I've done. I'm going to quit trying to do anything and from this point on I'm going to expect you to be the power and the source of everything that I do. I am not going to try to come up with my own answers about anything any longer. If you don't speak to my heart and tell me what to do, I'm not going to do anything."

Confidence in God's Healing Power

I put it just that bluntly, speaking from my heart. And at that moment I felt the presence of God in a strong way. It was about 11:30 at night, I was by myself walking down the street in Galveston with nobody around and I had a tremendous experience of the presence of God. It was such a powerful presence that it almost buckled my knees. And immediately I not only knew that God was very much with me, but I knew beyond any doubt that Esther would be completely healed. I knew with confidence, there was no question. It was just like it had already happened. I knew it was going to happen and it made no difference whether it happened now or in the future. I knew that it was as good as done and I started thanking the Lord for that.

I said: "Thank you, Lord, for healing Esther. I don't know when you are going to do it but I thank you for healing her because I know that it is going to happen." As I walked home I couldn't get over what had happened to me. It was a long time before I found out but I know now that it was the baptism of the Holy Spirit. And that first knowledge and confidence that my wife was going to be healed was the gift of faith, the miraculous gift of faith. It is one of the beautiful manifestations of the Spirit.

Within the next few days I began to experience other spiritual gifts. Again I didn't know what they were at the time; I only learned later. I began to experience the gift of knowledge and the gift of wisdom. I would find myself in situations where I was talking to a client and I suddenly knew some secret bit of information about his life that he had not told me. I would sit there listening, carrying on a conversation, wondering what to do with the secret. I knew it was from the Lord. Finally, after getting up some boldness, after maybe 15 or 20 minutes, I would share with my client what the Lord had told me about him. This happened several times, and that person would just fall apart because these secrets were always things they had not told to anyone and they knew it was the Lord who had revealed it to me. Since they were absolutely flabbergasted at the revelation, I would begin to share about my life with the Lord.

I saw and experienced all kinds of fruit from those charismatic gifts of knowledge and discernment. Other times the Lord would give me a supernatural revelation of the answer to some knotty problem that seemed hopelessly beyond solution. Suddenly, I would see the answer. I knew it could not be from me, because the answer was never typical of the way I usually solved problems or did things. As I shared these answers with people it would bring all kinds of peace and grace to a situation.

And so the Lord began to teach me about life in the Spirit in these ways.

Hunger for Scriptures

I found myself hungry for the scriptures. I had read the Scriptures before but now I just couldn't get enough of them. While I was reading in the Scriptures, the Lord would show me passages that explained things to me.

For a year and a half the Lord taught me this way. He taught me things out of the Scriptures that were so profound that it's still a shock to realize how he taught me so personally. He taught me about Satan's kingdom and the way that Satan works and then he would show me illustrations of that in the Scriptures. He would teach me how to pray about certain things. I would spend 45 minutes or so every morning just talking to him and reading the Scriptures. And then every night I would take anywhere from an hour to two hours walking and talking with the Lord.

Looking back I can see that during this period the Lord was making special provision for me before he put me into a community where he would later supply through people many of the things that he supplied to me directly. After a year and a half I began to meet other Christians who had been baptized in the Spirit, and I saw that I hadn't been getting off the track but that the Lord had been teaching me thoroughly and that I had been hearing him rightly. Praise him. In the end, I came into deep fellowship with those who became the Redeemer community. When I found the reality of fellowship with other spirit-filled Christians, it was just like coming home at the end of a hard day's work and finding a good supper waiting on the table and a loving wife. I knew I was home.

The other people felt the same way, particularly the five families who formed the core of the community at the Church of the Redeemer. The five men especially could not stay away from each other. We were drawn to each other like powerful magnets. Our five paths miraculously crossed within a few weeks and almost immediately we drew together and started meeting. At first, we met just a couple times a week, then three, four and five times a week. It got to be ridiculous because sometimes we drove 50 miles just to spend an hour together. I would get up early in the morning and drive to Houston just to spend some time of prayer and sharing with my brothers before I went to work. Finally after eight months of that kind of relating back and forth across two counties, we knew that the Lord was calling us all to move into Houston near the Church.

By this time Esther had been healed and baptized in the Spirit and all five of our children had been baptized in the Spirit. Within a period of nine months our five children received the baptism of the Spirit one after another. We didn't encourage them particularly: we just let them be and the Lord did it. Our teenaged children were the first. They saw so much life in my wife and me that they were drawn to it. They would ask questions and would want to go to the meetings that we were going to. It was a miraculous thing that the Lord did in bringing our whole family to a position of life in the Spirit.

Wife Healed of Illness

Since that night in Galveston when I had received the baptism of the Holy Spirit, I knew Esther would be healed. It was a year and a half before this healing became complete. Esther was able to return home after being in the hospital for only two and a half months. This in itself was a miracle. She made some slow progress at home but was still on medication heavily and seeing the psychiatrist twice a week. Then the Lord baptized her with the Holy Spirit. From that time she was completely symptom-free. The psychiatrist was absolutely astounded when he saw her. He stopped medication. Esther began to see him weekly; soon it was once a month and after a few more times we all knew there was no need for any more visits.

For exactly one year she was absolutely symptom-free. During this time all five of our children were baptized in the Spirit, and the Lord led us to move to Houston. That was a most fantastic year. My wife was so different I could hardly believe it. She was a girl I had never known before. I could hardly recognize her at times. She was so free, so loving, so full of grace.

After one year of special grace, the Lord started to work a deeper purification to make the changes permanent. He began to test her in all the old areas where she had been symptomatic before. He took her through one area at a time and had her work out her old sin responses in that area and get permanently free from them. A period of several years of real cleansing went on and, at the end, she was like she was during that year of complete grace when there were no symptoms. She no longer is symptomatic at all. She has a very strong and powerfully anointed life of faith. She functions as one of our "heavy ministers" both at our house and in the church. She is very effective in difficult situations and particularly with people who are emotionally disturbed.

Life in Community

Right now our life is lived in a deeply communal manner. It's a life that is unusual in many ways because the people who form part of it have made a deep commitment to the Lord and to his service. The core community at the Church of the Redeemer now numbers about 400 to 500 people living in over 30 community households. They have come together to live a life where the Lord is served and glorified.

I live in a household—we call them ministering communities—located in a black ghetto. Fourteen people live in our house; nine are black and five white. This group of people is living there because we all feel that we are called to a ministry to that neighborhood. It's a very depressed area with lots of poverty and many serious ghetto problems. I have my office in that same neighborhood. I practice law there along with a partner who is also committed to the Lord and a legal secretary who looks upon her job as service to the Lord. We approach our whole life in that office as a ministry. We try to be very good lawyers and to give good legal services—the best available. But we do it in the context of seeking to serve the whole man, dealing with the spiritual as well as the legal problems as it seems appropriate to do so.

At work we frequently minister faith to people just by talking to them about having faith in their situations. The Spirit anoints us to do this. We show people that God is really the God of their situations and that they will have his grace if they just turn to him and thank him for his faithfulness and love.

People experience precisely this grace and often emerge from that experience wanting to know more. This is often the beginning of a whole new life of faith for them. On the other hand, we don't hesitate to relate to people simply as lawyers to clients, not saying anything about the Lord's life. We are free to speak about the Lord or not to speak about him. We are free to hear the Lord in every situation and to respond to his word.

It is the same way at my home in the community where I live. Our life there is not one of carrying out a program. It is living the Christian life within a house in such a way that it can be seen and experienced by people in the neighborhood. The life we live is so remarkably different from that normally experienced in the world that the contrast is astonishing. Our life even threatens some people because it somehow convinces them that it is *possible* to live the Lord's life, that is is *possible* to love each other, that it is *really possible* to live by the power God has given to man to live by his Spirit.

Open House

We have open house every night and we encourage people to drop in just like friends visiting another friend's home. We gather in the living room and we visit about what's been going on in our lives. We share our lives by just sharing the things that the Lord is doing with us, the wonderful, miraculous little things that go on among us all the time. We share the Lord's work among us and his love for us. We relate everything to faith. We talk faith, we relate to each other in faith.

We openly love the people who come to the

house. We might shake hands with them when they come for the first time so that they're not caught off guard. But after talking with them briefly, we'll often openly embrace them with a big hug or something like that. This becomes a regular way of greeting; it is an expression of his love. People in the neighborhood expect to be hugged when they walk in the front door and they quickly learn to respond to that.

Many of the black people in the neighborhood have never had that kind of an intimate relationship with a white person or even with another black person. This way of relating across racial and cultural lines is very meaningful both for us and for them. We see that we are just an extension of the church in that neighborhood: all the other 33 houses that are doing other things of this sort are themselves this way too.

We believe that the Lord will anoint us to do everything he has called us to. We know and experience the way he gives us his love and faith, so it's not difficult for us to relate freely and openly to people. Some of the people in our house are from the immediate neighborhood and have become a full part of our community living. They have grown tremendously in the Spirit since they came.

So it goes. This is the kind of life I live. I practice law but I look upon my law practice and everything else I do as part of my service to the Lord and my commitment to him. There is no division in my life between the secular and the sacred. It's all sacred. All the laymen in our church are encouraged to regard their lives and their jobs this way. Whatever their work, it is done to serve the Lord, as an expression of their love for him. We approach our work in faith, with the attitude of serving God through it, with an attitude of reverence.

We find that it does not matter whether we see any particular results of our work in faith, because we do everything in every situation with the expectation that the Lord will communicate his life through us. If we work this way in faith, somehow his love, his peace, and his nature are revealed in any work, even though there might not be spiritual things said or the Lord's name mentioned. If a person is really living in faith, really committing his work into the Lord's hands, he finds that the Lord will shine forth one way or another and that work is not in vain.

To sum up, our life has been just full of surprises and full of fantastic things. There are just endless fantastic miracles that have happened to our family. These are miracles of every conceivable kind from miraculous medical healing to miraculous provision of food, money and furniture and automobiles, every conceivable thing. We have been living this life now since 1965. For six years we have constantly had other people with our natural family in our home. Very often we have had 14 or 15 people with us at one time. Our older children now have grown up into lives of real ministry and graceful living and service in the church community. My oldest son, Owen, is now functioning as an elder of the church, as well as pastor or head of one of the ministering houses—a very difficult role—in the hippie community. There have been many trials, many times of facing great temptations and spiritual battle, but it's been a life just full of grace and full of the Lord's peace. I have no end of thanks to him for what he has done.

PART II
Families and Community Life

I suppose my wife and I had been married approximately 20 years when I received the baptism of the Spirit. When we started coming together in terms of community, our family was well along the way in terms of years. Several of our children were already teenagers. Each of the other four families also had several children and the parents were people of approximately our age at the time—between 35-40 years old. One of them was our pastor, Graham Pulkingham, rector of the Church of the Redeemer. He had been there for a year before all of these things started happening. Another was a doctor, Dr. Eckert, a very successful general practitioner practicing about 35 miles from Houston. He had two offices in small towns and he was regarded as one of the up-and-coming young physicians of the area. Another was an engineer, Ladd Fields, who had been involved in a very technical kind of instrument field work for many years. And then there was a crew chief of a line crew for the power company, John Grimmet. He had worked for the power company for 25 years. All of us had families and we were all well-established people.

Very shortly after Esther received the baptism of the Spirit, I came across Graham. We discovered we had both been baptized in the Spirit and immediately started sharing. At that time Graham had been baptized in the Spirit exactly 30 days; I, for 18 months. The other men of the five families received the baptism of the Spirit just about that time and we began to gather together. The Lord put within our hearts an urgency to be together. We could see how precisely the Spirit of the Lord had picked us from the places where we were and chosen us to be a part of this particular undertaking. Very soon after we came together we began to get a sense about what the Lord was doing. He would encourage us. Practically anything we would pray for was answered almost instantly. It seemed impossible to get anything but a miraculous answer to prayer. All kinds of wild things would happen in our lives.

Moving Together

When the Lord began to speak to us about moving together into the neighborhood of the church, we were well prepared. For months we had been living a life that was shared in every way possible except geographically. By that time all our families were ready. The children were hungry for the life in the Lord. Our wives were sharing everything the men were sharing and they were a part of our gatherings whenever possible. Very often we would get free of our obligations and we'd get in the car and we'd run up to Houston to the church or over to Dr. Eckert's home. When we got there, we'd all pull our Bibles out and sit around the kitchen table or something like that and just start sharing what the Lord had been showing us and what had been happening in our personal lives. And you know, we'd just be awed at his majesty and grace, and we couldn't get over what he was doing to us.

I took several months to turn over files and things I was handling to my law partners and give up my law practice. Dr. Eckert closed out his medical practice. Ladd and John kept working in their jobs because they were near their work, but we all moved right into the neighborhood of the church. Any house we could get that was close was suitable. We hardly worried what it looked like. We all came from big, beautiful homes but that didn't matter anymore. We were there to share our life in the Lord. We had such anticipation. It was just like a kid on Christmas Eve; we were expecting anything. We didn't know what we were going to do. We just knew we were supposed to be there and we were supposed to be together in serving the Lord.

I began looking for a job, trusting that the Lord was going to give me some work. For three months I diligently looked in all places I ought to be looking, but I did not find anything. There were no jobs opening up. After a while I said, "Okay Lord, you know what you're doing." So I started doing a little work out at the house, things that people would bring to me, but it wasn't much. Mostly I just spent time helping Graham with the things that he needed.

At that time, troubled people were already coming to the church. The word had gotten around that the Church of the Redeemer was a place where people could get help. The day we moved into our house, we were joined by a confirmed alcoholic and a man who had spent most of the previous five years in mental hospitals. The day we moved in they moved in. Within another week, another mental case who was also an epileptic moved in. Then we got one or two younger men who were not really sick but who had just come to the Lord, been baptized in the Spirit, and needed to grow and be nurtured. Within no time at all seven other people were added to our household.

We started right away to live a community life. The men lived upstairs with my two older sons. The rest of the children, my wife and I, lived downstairs. We all ate together and we shared together. It was a community from the day we moved in. This was true of the other houses too. It was just the natural thing to do. People would come with needs and we'd know they couldn't be helped unless we took them right into our lives. We'd say, "come on over and live with us and believe the Lord with us." The Lord honored that beautifully. He was just so obviously pleased. When one of the mental cases would get violent we would ask the Lord to do something, and the Lord would miraculously do something immediately. There were several times when one fellow went completely out of his head and we asked the Lord to restrain him. Immediately the man was restrained against a chair or on the floor and couldn't move; he was literally bound there like an angel was holding him down or something. We wouldn't even touch him. He'd just be riveted to a chair or to the floor. We would see the powerful working of God's hand in those things and it encouraged us to ask him for impossible things.

Sharing Resources

Soon we naturally began to share our resources and to support people in our homes who had no resources or finances of their own. It became natural to share whenever anyone had a need. When somebody needed some furniture we'd share our furniture; if somebody needed a car we'd turn over our car to them. From the very beginning we began to share our possessions.

It soon became obvious that the needs we were

faced with would take lots of resources and so we began to cut expenses for things we had been accustomed to. We stopped buying new cars and new televisions and things of that sort. We didn't even think of them. We became interested in these possessions just for their utility value. We started driving our cars until they literally fell apart and then we'd buy a used car or something like that to replace it. We began to turn in some of our insurance policies so that they would not be such a financial drain on us. We found such a security in our relationship with the Lord that it was no longer important to have security for the future or protection against this or that and so eventually we gave up most of our insurance policies except something like liability insurance for our cars that we felt we should have. We never have had any rule about it or a feel that this is a necessary part of the Christian life. It was just a matter of using the money we had available most effectively, particularly in supporting so many extra people. We learned to live very economically. We quit eating steaks and expensive roasts and things like that and we began to eat simple fare. We found that when simple food is properly prepared it is pretty tasty. We'd often eat things that people would bring to us. People would bring us a box of groceries or a hundred pound sack of rice, or they would bring us a washing machine. Sometimes somebody would bring a hundred pounds of fish. We would put it in the deep freeze and supply all the houses with fish.

Before long, other people began to follow us. They began to join us in our life and to share those household ministries. More and more people began to join us in our regular gatherings, almost every day. We began to have services on Tuesday and Friday night and we were greatly blessed by the Lord. His presence was very strong.

Call To Service

I guess the main thing that happened with these families and with those that followed is that they became in every sense servants of God, ministers. We shared the ministry of that church in as full a way as Graham and the other ordained ministers. The really important thing that happened, though, was that the men and women and even the children became ministers. They had a sense of calling to lay everything down to serve the Lord in whatever ministry or service he had at hand to do.

After I had been working for a number of months in a legal aid office—the first job I got—the ministry became so heavy at the church that it became obvious that one of us was going to have to come and function in a full-time ministry. We all decided that the Lord was calling me to do that. I gave up the job and for a period of eight months I served as an assistant pastor of the church. During that time I grew a lot in knowing how to serve. I became very heavily involved in teaching and counseling; in putting people in homes and keeping track of what their needs were and how they were coming along; in seeing if the homes needed additional help in some way or another. I also helped to raise up the new people who were coming along and helped them to enter new responsibilities and service.

After working in a legal aid clinic and then directly in the church for eight months, the Lord very clearly spoke to me and told me to go back into law.

In those days, and it's still true, we never questioned the Lord about those things. We may not have necessarily understood why we were supposed to be doing those things but we just did it and the Lord blessed that. I established an office of my own and started functioning in a private practice. I had no money to pay a secretary so a woman from one of the houses who had had some experience as a secretary came with me. She had been in a terrible emotional condition and until this time had not been able to work. But she had been showing some improvement so I just brought her along and had her serve as my secretary. That was part of her healing. I would spend a certain amount of time every day just ministering to her to help her keep going. She functioned well as my secretary and as a result of that Christian work experience became very stable and strong and left there to take on a very responsible and high-paying legal secretary's job downtown. She has been working ever since.

Ministering the Lord's Life

All of the five original families which came in together in this life in the Lord unqualifiedly gave themselves to service. We really had no private life; we didn't want any. What we did was serve; we served at work, we served at home. We ministered the Lord's life at meal times, we ministered during the evening and sometimes we got up in the middle of the night to minister. It was not uncommon with problem cases to have to get up in the middle of the night and work with people and maybe stay up with them for the rest of the night. The women responded this way, the men responded this way, and as the children grew older the children began to respond this way. Some of the best and most dependable ministers I had in my house were my three older children, my two oldest sons and my daughter. You could absolutely depend upon them in critical situations. It was tremendous to see that coming forth in teenagers.

This was the beginning; and now it has spread to a church of 1200 people. Roughly 500 of these are deeply committed and deeply involved in community life, with about 400 actually living in ministering households. We have households of all shapes and sizes serving all kinds of functions and God just keeps on working. We can never thank and praise Him enough for the life He's given us.

Experience of a Son

By Owen Barker

Seven years ago our family was a very typical family, one in which there was lots of confusion, lots of clashing, lots of raw relationships. I have three brothers and one sister, all of us are pretty close together in age. I'm the oldest of the five. I grew up very close to my brother Conway who is a year younger than I am, but it was probably the most brutal relationship that either of us had. It was centered around a lot of competition and striving, bitterness and anger. It produced a whole lot of hurt. The younger kids, particularly my sister, were badly affected by the bad relationship between Conway and me. We would take it out on her. At this time I was seventeen years old. My mother had been in the hospital for a couple of months with a serious mental illness. At this point, my dad had been baptized in the Spirit about a year and a half but we didn't know what was going on with him.

For the few years before this, when I was fourteen through seventeen years old, our family was probably in its most pitiful state. I had pretty well decided that because of the hurt, the bitterness and the anger between my parents, it probably was not possible to have a happy, successful marriage. It really didn't seem to be right to have kids if that's the way you were going to bring them up. The relationship between my parents was so devastating to me that I figured it would be best if I could get away from them as much as possible. I certainly didn't think I had anything to learn from them.

The relationship with my brother was pretty bad at this point. We used to argue over which television programs to watch and then we'd go outside and fight until we were too tired to slug one another. Then we'd go in and pout in our corners and never would get the program that we wanted. It was a brutal relationship.

Then, in March of 1965, I went one evening to a litany service at the Church of the Redeemer. I had no particular reason for going except that our whole family was going and they invited me to go. I arrived there maybe 15 or 20 minutes late and my parents were sitting in the front row. I went on up to the front row and Graham Pulkingham, the pastor, was speaking. I don't remember what he said but I think that what really counted and had such an impact on my life was what I saw in the man. What I was seeing was the Lord's life. That life was full and powerful and complete. If the Lord could do that in him, I wanted him to do it in me, and I didn't care what the cost was. Then God began working in us.

The Lord began to nudge us very gently and we found ourselves falling in love with the Lord. We found ourselves hungering after the Lord and wanting to come to him. As soon as we were baptized in the Spirit, the Lord began to work on my relationship with Conway. One turning point came a week or ten days after we were baptized in the Spirit. I was going out and I had one of Conway's ties on. It was

his best tie and Conway is pretty particular about
his clothes and who wears them. It was a big thing
for him. He came down and saw me wearing his tie
and he demanded I take it off. I took it off and gave
it to him and he went storming up the steps to his
room. I put on another tie, but about four or five
minutes later he came storming down just weeping
and demanded that I take it back and wear it. That
was a big thing for him. It was a really big thing.

It wasn't that we decided to work out our relationship, we just saw the Lord begin to do it. Someone would say something that would offend the other
and then all of a sudden we'd just be crushed inside
and then we'd turn to the other and beg for forgiveness, or weep and pray with one another. That was a
real healing, a really big healing. Also, I can remember for the longest time I would try getting into
the Scriptures and it was just so dry. I'd fall asleep;
it was just terrible. I can remember in Galveston
going up to my dad's room early in the morning and
be so struck by an awesome awareness of the Lord's
presence as I found him praying. I'd open the door
and walk in and it was all I could do to stop from
saying, "Excuse me, Lord, but dad, could I have this
or that?" It was like walking in on Moses praying.
Seeing my father with the Lord like that drew me,
you know, it really drew me. He not only had his
nose in the Word, he was sensing a real deep hungering to talk to God. He didn't tell us that, you know,
but we saw it. We saw this going on each morning.
He'd get up at 4:30 in the morning and go out on the
front porch. Before long my mother was out there.
Then Cheryl was out there. Then I was out there and
Conway was out there. We didn't know anything

about the Bible but we'd open it and the Lord would show us things.

We saw the Lord working in each one of us in the family, and in dad particularly. The love that I saw for the first time between my parents made me wish that I could have a marriage like that. And I knew, if the Lord could do it in them, he could do it in us. If the Lord could speak to my dad like that, he could speak to us. Dad would go out on a walk in the evening sometimes for an hour. The rest of us would eagerly wait for him to come back just to find out what the Lord was saying to him. All of this was just feeding and building our faith. It was giving us the assurance, "my people, I love you. I want to be with you. I want to talk with you. I want to hold you. I want you to be my people. I want to be your God." It was exciting to find this new life unfolding within us.

On Saturdays we would drive 35 miles to Dr. Eckert's house and spend the whole day teaching and worshipping and eating together in fellowship. One day we all prayed and together asked the Lord to heal my wrist, which had just been broken badly and put in a cast. It was supposed to take three months to heal. Two weeks later I felt the Lord was asking me to take the cast off, and three days later it was back to normal size and in perfect shape and I've never had any trouble from it since. With things like that the Lord encouraged and strengthened us.

Sometimes our family would go to Hitchcock together—40 miles away—and have almost an hour together in the car. We'd drive together worshipping in the Spirit and the gifts of the Spirit would be operating. We were 17, 16, 14 years old and as we asked the Lord to express and manifest this new life, we'd experience the gifts of wisdom and knowledge, prophecy and healing operating in our midst. It was so much better than what we had had before we appreciated the love of Jesus that we wanted to stay in it no matter what the cost was. This enthusiasm and zeal has never left us.

From there we moved into Houston in June of 1965, the same year all this happened. The first day we had an alcoholic and two men with very serious mental problems move in. One of them was an epileptic. From that day until this, we've been living in households dedicated to the service of God and enjoying the love and joy of his life and the power of his working in ever deeper ways.

A Different Brand
of Medicine

By Bob Horning

A 19-year-old girl saw Dr. Bob Eckert walk into the clinic as she was waiting for an appointment. "Look doctor, I'm clean," she said. When Dr. Eckert didn't recognize her right away, she explained, "A year ago you treated me for heroin abscesses. You told me about a new life and asked me if you could pray for me. I said you could.

"You prayed that God would speak to me because it would take a word from him to change my life. When I left, I thought you were the kookiest doctor in the world. I went home, filled the rig, and had the needle in the vein, when God said, 'No, not anymore!' Somehow I knew it was God speaking. I haven't had a fix or a pill of any kind since."

This is the type of thing that has happened since Dr. Eckert started a medical clinic in Houston's most concentrated ghetto six years ago. About 7,000 poor or near-poor persons, mostly black, live in the eight-by-ten block area of Houston's Fourth Ward. The clinic offers free crisis and long-term comprehensive care to the neighborhood.

But, as Dr. Eckert says, "We're not here to doctor. We're here to share the Lord Jesus. The medical practice is something that comes out of the love God has for people. Our calling is to be medical people and return the life that God gives us, not only to our patients but to our profession." One employee said, "We are not here to get things done, but to be involved in people's lives however they need us to be involved."

"It is through love," Dr. Eckert says, "that the patients' lives are opened so there can be a change in their relationship with God, with people, and in their health."

The clinic has helped hundreds like the 19-year-old girl to experience a change in their lives. Some are delivered from drug addiction; some from alcoholism; some are healed physically through prayer; some receive counsel for family, personal, or spiritual problems. All see the work and the love and know that it is from God.

To be exposed to the atmosphere of the clinic is important for ghetto people, Dr. Eckert feels. "A person who is raised in poverty in a ghetto situation usually has a soul that is as impoverished as his surroundings. That person has no vision for anything other than poverty; he has no vision about how hopeless he is. He doesn't even realize that he has a hopeless feeling."

Eckert describes the clinic as a chance for "God to bring hope into hopeless lives. The main thing I have seen happen in the ghetto is for that hopelessness to change into hope. People are beginning to get jobs, get married, stop having illegitimate children. They are eating meals instead of merely putting cookies on the table all day long. Spiritual change is bringing about a change in the soul and body."

Workers at the clinic feel their mission is to bring life to the patients by giving God's life to them. This can mean spending an hour counseling with patients at the clinic or on the phone, or taking a patient home if he needs a place to stay.

Because of the atmosphere of love in the clinic, many patients are open to being prayed with before or after treatment, and some ask for prayers themselves. Others come to the clinic just for prayer or counsel.

The presence of love is what enables lives to be changed. "Almost no patients thank us for the medical care," Dr. Eckert says. "But they thank us for what we are to them, for being there. They know there is going to be more going on than medical care. The thanks for medicine is wrapped up in the other thanks. They see not only the free service offered, but the love going on among the employees; this love overflows to the patients. Something happens between us and patients—we enter into a brotherhood together."

Perhaps two patients will become Christians each month through someone at the clinic talking and praying with them, Dr. Eckert estimates. The number is not very high, he says, because most of the patients are already Christians. "This may not be obvious because the practice of righteousness in their lives is pretty poor compared to what you and I might expect of a Christian, but they haven't been raised in as much light as we have.

"In ways of trusting God in their hardships, though, they are way beyond us. Many are in a devastated walk of Christianity; their souls are devastated. But many return to a walk with Christ through the clinic."

The people at the clinic believe that there is a limit beyond which a basically white clinic in a black neighborhood can't penetrate. The cultural and religious differences prevent a complete integration. Dr. Eckert thinks that it would take 10-20 years of living in the ghetto before a white clinic or household could have full relationship with people in the ghetto. Still, they are able at present to draw people into the life of love at the clinic, and let them see a different way of living, let them see the possibility of change, the hope.

The financial policy of the clinic is another way of showing God's love, and demonstrates God's care for his people. A sign in the waiting room reads, "We are a private, non-funded clinic; a patient will receive no bill. He can pay what he is able and inclined."

The government and Model Cities program have offered money to support the clinic, but Eckert doesn't feel the Lord wants them to operate that way. He said God told him, "If you look to the needs of the people, I will look to your needs. Give to whomever I send, as I have given freely to you. You don't have to ask for anything. Ask me."

Monthly income and expenditure for the clinic is $20,000. Seventy percent of the income comes from government welfare insurance, such as Medicare or Medicaid. The rest is from donations and from the patients who are able to pay their bills. Thousands of dollars for equipment, furniture, and expansion, which isn't included in the $20,000, have been given to the clinic.

Since opening the clinic, God has supplied all the needs. At first there was only Dr. Eckert, two other workers, a desk, a table, and Eckert's black bag. Four patients came the first day, seven the next, and then the number steadily increased as people heard about the place. Always Eckert had in his bag whatever the patients needed.

Over the next six weeks, people who heard about the clinic completely furnished the three rooms and lab with furniture and equipment. Six nurses began to work one day a week, along with a receptionist—who soon got a chair—and a lab technician.

Today there are 100 employees, including four full-time doctors and 12 part-time. About 100-200 patients are served each day.

When the clinic was moved into its present building, a former supermarket, the owner of the supermarket was so impressed with the clinic operation and personnel that he gave them free rent for six months, and $40,000 towards converting the supermarket into a clinic. The president of the market's realty company publicly said that his life hasn't been the same since the first day of talking to the people at the clinic.

An incident with the Black Panthers of Houston illustrates how the needs of the clinic are met if they first supply the needs of others. The Black Panthers began a program in the ghetto of escorting senior citizens to the bank to cash their checks so they wouldn't get robbed along the way. The Panthers didn't have transportation, however, so they asked for help from the clinic. After talking it over, the clinic administrators decided to buy them a car. They contacted a Ford dealer and bought a station wagon for $1,000. When the Panthers received it, they couldn't believe it. One of them said, "This place (the clinic) has become a beacon of hope for the neighborhood."

The Ford dealer was also impressed and began getting more involved with the nearby Episcopal Church of the Redeemer. A month later he gave the clinic a new pick-up truck.

Dr. Eckert says, "We are not needy. We may have needs, but we are not needy. God supplies."

It was Dr. Eckert's medical practice immediately before starting the clinic that made him see the need for a free-give clinic. He had worked for three years with other physicians who charged a comparatively low rate, but still there were many people refused treatment, or unable to buy a prescription because they couldn't afford it. He began to sense the Lord calling him to a free-give medical practice.

Now the clinic provides many things that are usually only found in a hospital, but which clinic patients couldn't afford. They have a pharmacy that dispenses free medicine. Before, patients would get a prescription from the clinic but not have the money to go to a hospital or drug store to get it filled.

The clinic laboratory does as much work per day as a 200-bed hospital. While a patient is waiting to see a doctor for one thing, he might have general lab work done free. The patient's ability to pay doesn't restrict extra work being done for him. Eckert says that since God supplies their needs, they are free from relating to the patient financially.

One of the reasons the clinic is able to charge nothing and pay low wages is that most of the employees live together in a number of households. They form a community centered around the medical profession, and are dedicated to its renwal. Those living in the households support one another financially, physically, and spiritually. They share their money, their possessions, and the work around the house. There are about 80 members, including children, in the eight households.

The medical community is a little over a year old and was started by Dr. Eckert and others who had experience in communal living at the Church of the Redeemer. It is nondenominational, though a majority of the members are Episcopalian.

None of the physicians receive a salary. Those working full-time earn enough by working in another doctor's office. Those working part-time have their own private practices. The other employees likewise require little pay because of their household living.

The atmosphere of the clinic is not outwardly Christian or evangelistic. There are no banners, crosses, or sermons given. There is no coaxing of the patients toward a deeper spiritual life. Yet, when patients and visitors enter, they know God is present. Many visitors who take the Friday afternoon tour weep because they see people in need and see God meeting their needs through the prayer and work of the employees. They leave encouraged, knowing what God can do in a person's life.

Charles Foss, assistant administrator of the clinic, says, "It is important for those of us who work here to witness to Christ by simply being ourselves. Being spiritual doesn't mean we have to be in church all day praising God or to be constantly letting others know we are Christians.

"The Lord has most of us in the world. We are to be in the middle of life, of suffering, need, poverty. By being real 20th century people in Houston,

Texas, God's glory is being shown forth in the clinic. We don't have to worry about our testimony or about winning souls. We are learning to be gracious in proclaiming the Gospel, so we don't turn people off. As long as we are faithful to be where the Lord asks us to be, as long as we are willing to work hard in the nitty-gritty situations, then it is God's responsibility to show forth his glory to the world."

Besides the mission of serving patients at the clinic, Dr. Eckert feels God has an additional goal in mind. About two and a half years ago he was given a vision for renewal of the entire medical profession. The clinic and medical community are the first of many similar set-ups Dr. Eckert believes God is planning for Houston and other cities. He sees the community as a launching pad for a more powerful ministry in the field of medicine. The clinic plays a major part in this.

Clinic workers have had many opportunities to share what the Lord is doing among them. Dr. Eckert himself, besides heading the clinic, is an instructor at Baylor College of Medicine, on the staff of St. Joseph Hospital, and a member in good standing of the Harris County Medical Society. The other doctors are also affiliated with hospitals in Houston and other medical groups.

Wherever medical community people go, they "happen" to meet doctors, nurses, and "happen" to be able to share with them about the clinic, Foss says. Doctors that are alcoholics or that dislike their jobs are invited to come to the clinic and get a new vision of the medical practice.

Dr. Eckert hopes to publish a medical journal soon, combining theory and theology of Christian medical practice with the experience and insights that have been gained at the clinic, and that can be used elsewhere. Already there are clinics similar to that of the Fourth Ward being started in nearby towns, and more are anticipated.

The clinic serves as a place for others to observe a different kind of practice, to get a vision, teaching, and practical wisdom on how to set up their own clinic.

Personnel also train students from Houston schools and hospitals, and Dr. Eckert travels to speak to medical people who are interested in establishing similar clinics.

When other medical people visit the clinic or see the community way of living, it can have a profound influence on their life and practice. One night the international director of a company that sells lab equipment came to the Sunday night public worship meeting of the community and came into a new relationship with the Lord. The next day he gave $60,000 worth of new medical equipment to the clinic.

About two years ago, the president of the county medical society saw the clinic operation and said it is the perfect practice of medicine. "This is the way it should be done, and once was done in the country," he said. "The philosophy is right."

"Is That Your School Across the Street?"

By Fr. Jeff Shiffmayer

Nine years ago, shortly after she moved to Houston, Betty Jane Pulkingham, our rector's wife, said she had a strong feeling that someday the Lord would bring Lantrip Elementary School and the Church of the Redeemer closely together. Certainly the two buildings were physically close; Lantrip is right across the street. Over the years, many of our visitors have asked us, "Is that your school across the street?" The question has become a familiar one.

Members of the church made little attempts over the years to get involved. These attempts included joining the P.T.A., tutoring a few Spanish-American children to help them to catch up on their English, and helping some of the troubled children to overcome some of their emotional problems. However, no doors opened and our involvement was very insignificant until early September, 1971, when the busing program to integrate Houston's schools began.

A number of the children in Lantrip, which was primarily white and Mexican-American, were exchanged with a number of black children from a nearby elementary school. This exchange seemed to bring up the sins of everybody involved: the teachers, the white students, the black students, and the Mexican-American students. Lantrip School quickly became a serious spiritual battleground, with the children as pawns. Our children came home daily, traumatized by spiritual, emotional, and physical threats. Regularly parents would have to spend an hour or more soothing and strengthening their children after school. Our children were getting into fights and being beaten up. They were terribly upset and felt guilty about the sin that came up in their own hearts.

Terrific pressure mounted on the parish over the course of the school year and we got into a real soul-searching. Did the Lord want us to keep our children in that school? Were we making our children some kind of sacrifice that was not his will? After much discussion and prayer, the consensus was that the children might be able to get a better intellectual education elsewhere. But we felt that the children would learn much about the life of the Son of God if we were to stand our ground and trust God to show us how to take charge over the situation.

However, weeks and months passed and nothing seemed to open up. We had many discussions with the school principal about the need for some kind of change. Neither he nor we could see how change was supposed to happen.

Then one night, just a few weeks before the end of the school year, the Elders of the church concluded one of our many discussions about the problem by directing me to call Mr. Roberts, the principal, the next morning. I was to tell him that we were willing to pull people out of the various ministries in the parish and send them over to Lantrip. They would monitor the school grounds before and after school and during the recess periods, and do anything else that would put a body of responsible spiritual people in the middle of that warfare.

The next morning I came to church ready to call Mr. Roberts and to my surprise found a telephone message on my desk saying, "Jeff, call Mr. Roberts as soon as you get to your office this morning." When I called he told me that a man from the Houston School District headquarters was in his office to talk about a new program called Volunteers in Public Schools (VIPS). The purpose of this program was to draw concerned neighborhood adults into the dynamics of the local schools, hoping to introduce stabilizing elements into all the schools of the city, and to somehow make the education of the children more of a corporate, citywide community endeavor. The VIPS man wanted to know if some people from the Church of the Redeemer would like to get involved in the program. He had heard that our parish was dynamic and deeply involved in social programs. I was astonished at God's goodness in opening up the door with such split-second timing after nine years of waiting.

We immediately got involved driving and riding buses and monitoring the school grounds. But we looked to the summertime to mobilize for a major involvement in the school for the coming 1972-73 school year. This year we have been able to supply 38 adults to Lantrip School on a regular basis.

They are men and women who were involved in homes, in other schools, and in other kinds of jobs. Their primary concern is to be an effective arm of the Body of Christ. If the Lord was calling this Body to give its love and energy to Lantrip School, they wanted to be involved in that work. They were offering themselves, their talents, their education, their time.

When we called for people to help at the school, I was astonished at the variety and appropriateness of the gifts of the people who came forth. They had gifts of music and song, in sports, in teaching English as a second language. A number had professional experience as regular teachers and special education teachers. Some of these teachers left full-time jobs in fine schools in Houston to become nonpaid volunteers in Lantrip School. Their primary concern was to serve the Lord. They knew that their own financial needs and the needs of others would be met in other ways in the Body. Of course they put their teaching careers on the line by leaving promising situations to take up what looked like a thankless job in a little-known school.

I was convinced that the Lord wanted us to have the janitor's position and the position of the school secretary—both key positions in the school. Since the school had a janitor and a secretary, all we could do was offer our candidates for those jobs and pray. The last week of school, both the janitor and the secretary surprised school officials by announcing their retirements. Our candidates were hired. A young man is the janitor, and a woman who speaks English and Spanish is the secretary.

Members of the parish serve Lantrip School in many ways. Young people ride the buses, play the guitar, and teach the children songs to distract them from the temptations to tease, fight, and cause bedlam in the buses. Others have been hired as fulltime paid staff, and some are assistant teachers working with the most troubled youths in the classroom. Some of these children were in the fourth grade and could not even write their own names, not because they were mentally deficient, but because they were emotionally so torn up that they were unable to learn. But in the context of an intimate and loving relationship with an adult—day after day, week after week, month after month—they found great healing in their lives and the ability to carry on normal school work. Some of them are now performing at better than average levels, while most are progressing along with the class.

Some of the students now finding healing in their lives were previously involved with drugs and some with prostitution. Many of them have met the Lord and are learning to pray about their own problems. This has brought about healing between the children and some of their parents, and between the parents and the Lord Jesus.

Many of the Lantrip staff have taken new courage from this spiritual revolution. Some had been strong Christians, but had been overcome by the situation in the school. For example, the bus driver could not believe the change. This man had been driving the bus practically at the risk of his own life, often delivering children at the end of their bus rides with bloody noses and torn clothing. He was overcome by the spirit of peace and love that settled on the bus as our guitarist taught the children songs and talked to them and helped them with their emotional problems. As the children left the bus the second day, saying good-by to the bus driver and smiling at him he could barely contain himself until the last child had been dropped off. At that point, he burst into tears and, with anguish and awe in his voice, said to the young guitarist, "What is going on here? What is happening?"

Another incident occurred last fall. Two days before school was to start, the janitor needed to put in 600 man-hours of cleaning for inspection. He brought his request to the Tuesday praise and teaching meeting. In two days, volunteers had finished the cleaning.

Over the next seven weeks, 2,000 more man-hours of help were put in. Walls and windows were washed, floors waxed, trees planted, hedges trimmed.

A change in attitude accompanied the physical change at Lantrip. The principal, instead of despairing at the rundown condition of his school, now talks about one day having the showplace school of the district. One of the teachers who had been especially bitter about the school, wept when he saw a group of workers cleaning his room.

For follow-up work, each Saturday a team from church maintains the school. As a result, many teachers have decided to plan improvements for their rooms.

Recently a reporter from Minnesota, here to visit the Church of the Redeemer, decided to visit Lantrip on his own to see just how much of an impact our 38 people were really having on the school. He walked onto the school grounds, and went up to two little black boys, who were standing and talking in the yard. He asked, "Hey kids, what do you know about that church across the street?" One of the little boys immediately responded, "Oh, they love us!"

To me, this is the testimony of the Son of God who has healing in his wings.

The entire atmosphere of the school has changed. It changed so radically that the Center for Human Resources Development and Educational Renewal (CHARD) office of the Houston Independent School District has a desire to implement our "program" throughout the entire district. The VIPS program has invited members of our ministry to be on the board of VIPS as exemplar representatives of their "adopt-a-school" plan.

I see a basic principle operating in this situation: when a body of people respond together to the Lord's call to become involved in some social evil, the strength, depth, and generosity of their mutual relationships keep them free, open, and life-giving. Thus, together, through a variety of gifts, they are able to inject life into a poisonous situation. At the same time, they are able to invite people, poisoned by the situation, into the fellowship that brings them spiritual healing. This fellowship is really the presence of the risen Lord among his people.

Notes on the Contributors

Bob Horning is a member of the *New Covenant* editorial staff.

Kerry Koller is a leader in the San Francisco community and also serves as a member on the North American Service Committee.

Steve Clark is a coordinator of The Word of God in Ann Arbor, Michigan, a member of the North American Service Committee and author of several books including *Building Christian Community*. This article is adapted from a talk given in February 1974 in Bogotá, Columbia, at the second Latin American Catholic Charismatic Meeting (ECCLA).

Fr. James Burke was a Dominican missionary in Bolivia for a number of years. While there he was the rector of the major theological seminary in La Pax, superior of the Dominican Fathers of Bolivia, and co-founder of IBEAS, the Bolivian Institute of Social Study and Action. He is now doing charismatic retreat work in North and South America.

Fr. Rick Thomas, S.J., is director of Our Lady's Youth Center, serving one of the poorer sections of El Paso, Texas. He leads prayer groups in El Paso and in Juarez, Mexico, across the river.

Cindy Conniff is on the *New Covenant* editorial staff.

Sir Thomas and Lady Lees are active in their church, where Tom is a lay reader, an ecumenical officer for the Diocese of Salisbury, and a member of the General Synod of the Church of England. He and Faith have four children.

Kevin Perrotta is a member of The Word of God in Ann Arbor, Michigan, and served as a guestmaster for several years.

Louise Bourassa is on the *New Covenant* editorial staff.

Maynard Howe has labored as a missionary for many years in Canada, western United States and in Mexico.

James D. Manney is on the *New Covenant* editorial staff. He is also author of the book, *Aging in American Society*, published by the U.S. Government Printing Office.

Pete Perona is a leader in the New Vine community in Detroit, Michigan made up largely of young people.

R. Douglas Wead is an Assemblies of God minister. He is the author of many books, including *Tonight They'll Kill a Catholic*, a story of love and hate in Northern Ireland.

Maria F. von Trapp, daughter of the Baroness Maria von Trapp, has been a missionary to New Guinea since 1956.

Capt. T. David Parham is a naval chaplain stationed at the Naval Training Center, Bainbridge, Maryland. He also serves on the executive committee of the Council on Discipleship and Worship for the Presbyterian General Assembly. The article is a condensation of a talk given at the Third International Presbyterian Conference on the Holy Spirit in February 1974.

Fr. Charles Magsam is an American missionary working in Talcahuano, Chile. He participated in Chile's first charismatic conference in February 1972.

Gary Seromik in on the *New Covenant* editorial staff and works with the International Communication Office.

Jerry Barker, his wife Esther, and their five children are members of the Church of the Redeemer, a charismatically renewed Episcopalian parish in Houston, Texas. Part of the family is now working for the renewal in England, as an outreach from Church of the Redeemer. This article describes the renewal of their family and the life they experience as part of a community.

Owen Barker, Jerry Barker's oldest son, lives and serves in the Church of the Redeemer in Houston, Texas.

Fr. Jeff Schiffmayer is pastor of the Episcopal Church of the Redeemer in Houston, Texas, a parish which has become widely known as a center for charismatic renewal. Redeemer's ministries include a medical clinic, a legal aid program, and the Fishermen, an organization which helps other churches open to renewal.